Authenticated by the Donald A. Hall Estate

Donald A. Hall

Chief Engineer ~ 1927 ~ Spirit of St. Louis

TM

"To Donald . . .

We never met and yet
you've always been with me in spirit.
With love and dedication,
this book is my testament to you.

Your loving grandson."

The men and women of Ryan Airlines, Inc. who designed and built the Spirit of St. Louis in sixty days.

Spirit & Creator

THE MYSTERIOUS MAN BEHIND LINDBERGH'S FLIGHT TO PARIS

BY NOVA HALL

FIRST EDITION

Book and jacket design by Pakaáge (http://www.pakaage.com)

Library of Congress Cataloging-in-Publication Data

Hall, Nova
   Spirit & Creator / Nova Hall
      p. cm.
   ISBN 0-9702964-4-4
      1. Aviation history 2. Hall, Donald A. 3. Lindbergh 4. Photography

Library of Congress Control Number: 2003102261

ATN Publishing, 561 Shunpike Rd., Sheffield, MA 01257 (413) 229-7935

CONTENTS

Spirit & Creator

THE MYSTERIOUS MAN BEHIND LINDBERGH'S FLIGHT TO PARIS

PREFACE

THE FUNDAMENTAL QUALITIES THAT ALLOWED THE DESIGNING AND BUILDING OF THE SPIRIT OF ST. LOUIS — hard work, teamwork, dedication, and an unwillingness to accept anything less than success — are qualities that every human being possesses. Whether or not we choose to put these qualities of greatness to use is, however, up to each of us. Donald Hall, the *Spirit's* talented designer, and Charles Lindbergh, the aviator with a dream, weren't satisfied with watching others make history. Instead, they took action. In doing so, they changed the course of aviation history. Perhaps more importantly, their spirit of excellence set an example for us and for future generations.

That optimistic human spirit is evident in the Pulitzer prize-winning book, "The Spirit of St. Louis," that Charles Lindbergh wrote about his experiences as the pilot who flew the *Spirit* into the annals of history. No such book was written by my grandfather, Donald A. Hall, the man who created the unique aircraft and who certainly shared Lindbergh's optimistic and pioneering spirit. More focused on design than on public relations, Donald Hall turned his attention to creating new aircraft. So, the young aeronautical engineer soon slipped from the spotlight that was trained firmly on the charismatic and photogenic young pilot.

Yet, I believe we can learn from and be inspired by the Donald Hall story. My hope is that this book will once more shine the spotlight on the man whose hard work, teamwork, dedication, and unwillingness to accept mediocrity made the *Spirit of St. Louis* a success. In SPIRIT AND CREATOR, you will experience the creation of the *Spirit* from the perspective of its designer and learn about Donald Hall, the conservationist, photographer, athlete, and family man.

It is my hope that SPIRIT AND CREATOR will not only honor my grandfather, Donald Albert Hall, but will commemorate the sixty-day experiment that opened a new chapter in aviation and the formation of a lifelong friendship between two men who had faith in the sky and insubstantial air. ⬎

— Nova Hall, GRANDSON

FOREWORD

Having been born after Charles A. Lindbergh crossed the Atlantic Ocean in the Spirit of St. Louis, I grew up building model airplanes and reading every publication available on this man and his flights. As I continued my deep interest in aviation, I was always reminded who Charles Lindbergh was and what he had contributed. He was an American hero, adopted around the world as the man of the century.

But it was not until many years later that I heard of Donald Albert Hall and his connection to the success of that flight to Paris in 1927 and his friendship with the famous aviator. Donald Hall seldom appeared in periodicals and books on aviation except as the Ryan Airlines engineer who worked out the technical details for the design and building of the *Spirit of St. Louis.* I wondered why.

Years later, as a pilot, I continued to read books and magazines on aviation. I began to notice that the authors often seemed to differ in their writing about Lindbergh or the famous airplane. I

eventually felt that someone should take the time to carefully research the subject and tell the story correctly, accurately, and thoroughly. With strong encouragement from friends, I took on the job.

My research into the early years of the Ryan company (Ryan Airlines, Inc., and later the Ryan Aeronautical Company), began to fill my files with technical data, photographs, and stories on the *Spirit of St. Louis.* During these years, my mind often turned to thoughts of Donald A. Hall and many of the other Ryan people who played such important roles in the creation of that airplane. However, when it came time for me to dig deeper into who Donald Albert Hall was and where he came from, there was little information.

As I continued to write my book, "The Untold Story of the Spirit of St. Louis," I intensified my detective work on the *Spirit's* engineer, eventually making contact with the Hall family. Hall's son, Don Hall, Jr., grandson Nova Hall, and I developed a pleasant friendship, just as Charles Lindbergh and Donald Albert Hall had become friends in 1927. We happily shared our mutual interest in the *Spirit of St. Louis* and the men who had brought about its creation.

I was pleased to learn sometime later that Nova was planning to write a book about Donald A. Hall. The time had finally arrived to honor the man and give him the credit he had earned and deserved. Who better to write such a book than his own grandson? I read the manuscript with more than a casual interest, having spent over 35 years in the research of the complete history of the *Spirit of St. Louis.* In the process, I feel I have gotten to know Donald Hall intimately. This long overdue book is a tribute to a wonderful and talented gentleman.

Nova Hall has certainly inherited the "Spirit" from Donald Albert Hall. He has come as close as humanly possible, 75 years later, to telling precisely who his grandfather was. A unique and refreshing work, SPIRIT AND CREATOR is well written, complete, honest, informative, and accurate. In its pages you will find the record of a man who achieved a short-lived success in the annals of aviation history. His little-known career was without flamboyance, theatrics, legerdemain, or luck. He never compromised his integrity for the lure of quick gain or eventual profit.

Hall, a soft-spoken, conscientious, and intelligent gentleman, took on the *Spirit of St. Louis* project with enthusiasm, dedication, and ability. He worked out the details, the calculations, and the design to make each pound of fuel carry a given load the maximum number of miles, insuring the greatest degree of safety and reliability to fly the *Spirit* non-stop across an entire ocean. His accomplishment required fundamental knowledge and analytical power in the field of both fluid and solid mechanics such as were to be found, in general, only in the university atmosphere.

SPIRIT AND CREATOR is the story of a gifted man lost to history over the years, a man who contributed much to the success of one of the most magnificent events in American aviation. Through this work, Donald Albert Hall will finally be recognized and remembered by present and future generations of students and scholars of aviation history.

I recommend this book to all who are curious about how Donald Hall contributed to the creation of the *Spirit of St. Louis* and to those with an interest in the friendship between this talented engineer and the incredible aviator, Charles A. Lindbergh. This story should revive many memories for us, inducing a sense of nostalgia for American aviation history, along with renewed admiration and respect for the man who helped make the 1927 achievement possible. ✐

— Ev Cassagneres
Spirit of St. Louis Expert, AVIATION HISTORIAN

ACKNOWLEDGMENTS

THIS BOOK HAS ENCOMPASSED THE COMBINED WORK, DEVOTION, AND SPIRIT OF MANY PEOPLE. The *Spirit & Creator* team encompasses several individuals. The greatest supporter has been my father, Don Hall, Jr. Without his wisdom, knowledge, constant guidance, and eternal friendship, this book would not have happened. I also offer my heartfelt thanks to my friend and business partner, David J. Pashman, who acted as *2002 Spirit 75th* project administrator and personal advisor to the *Spirit & Creator* production, and to editor Sandi Corbitt-Sears for her literary vision. I am especially grateful to Diane Papadakis (Pakaáge) for her beautiful book design, unending devotion to this project, and design usage of my grandfather's handwriting to grace the chapter introductions.

Special acknowledgment goes to the men and women of Ryan Airlines and to Charles A. Lindbergh for making the *Spirit's* flight possible and for always believing in my grandfather. The impossible became possible in their grand experiment. To Gene Lyle, thank you for always being such a good friend to my grandfather.

Thank you, my entire family, for moral guidance and sometimes blunt advice. You have kept me on the straight and narrow with compassion. To Grandma and Grandpa, I will always remember the love you two gave me and the Chanukahs and Thanksgivings we spent together. For Sylvia, Ralph, Jon, Zoe, and Mom — I love you all. To my Aunt Ruth and the memory of my great uncle, David Klein.

I wish to give credit to these organizations that have taught me so much about life and business: Toastmasters of Sedona; Alternative Health Networks, Inc.; and Verde Valley School, my college-preparatory high school in Sedona, Arizona. I would also like to extend my thanks to the following persons: our aviation editor, Kermit Weeks; the wonderful and helpful staff at the Lindbergh Foundation; Don Wiegand who selflessly helped us during difficult days; and the numerous friends and supporters whom we met for the first time in Long Island and Washington, D.C. — thank you.

I extend gratitude to my great aunt Nellora Walker, who has helped to inspire this book with solid action; Justin Frankel for trusting in me; and Nina Anderson and Stephen Hawkins for making this book a reality. To my mentors, Thom Dougherty, Jeff Perkins (a great photography teacher), John Griffiths, and Doug Gettler, thank you for your support. Gratitude also goes to my good friends Bryan Burton for believing in me, Jez Gaddoura for the *Spirit 75th*, Mary Helmig for her love and support. Thank you to Samuel & Ann Louis Smith, Omar Walker, Louise & Malcolm Dunn, Ev Cassagneres, Ken Wiederhorn, Sheldon Harrison, Erik Lindbergh, Morgan Lindbergh, Reeve Lindbergh, Daniel E. Sears, Gail Weaver Mello, Manuel P. Papadakis, Ty Sundstrom, Tony Moreno, Dan Clemons, Bill Channa, Greg Godek, David Reiter, Antoinette Kuritz, Joe Durepos, Will Montague, the San Diego Aerospace Museum, the Smithsonian, the National Lindbergh 75th Anniversary Committee, the Donald A. Hall Aviation Foundation, and the Lindbergh Foundation. I extend a special thank you to the people of France for the ongoing opportunities to celebrate this historic anniversary in your country. May Paris & New York City remain sister cities in this celebration and for many years to come.

Lastly, I feel I must acknowledge the tragedy that occurred on September 11, 2001, during the compilation of this book. All aviation mourned that day. May this book honor the spirit of flight that has inspired aviators for decades while we mourn the tremendous losses of that fateful day. ✎

INTRODUCTION

My grandfather passed away in 1968, eight years before I was born, so what I knew of him was limited to family stories. I learned about him not as a gifted aeronautical engineer, but as a man who loved to hike among the tall pines in the Cuyamaca Mountain wilderness near San Diego. I knew Donald A. Hall had done something important, but I felt removed from him and from that titanic event in American history. Occasionally, I would ask about my grandfather's connection to the *Spirit of St. Louis*, but there it would stop. I was young and more interested in surfing, swimming, and current aviation than in the aeronautical events of the past.

In 1998, five years after moving to Sedona, Arizona, my father received a letter that would change all that. Historian Ev Cassagneres was writing a book about the *Spirit of St. Louis* and had been looking for my grandfather's only son, Don Hall, Jr., for a quarter of a century. He had located my great aunt in San Diego, California, and she agreed to contact my father for the author. A meeting was arranged, and Cassagneres flew from Connecticut to interview us. He had been researching the *Spirit* for 35 years and hoped we could provide answers to lingering questions about Donald Hall's part in building the aircraft.

What he told us about my grandfather's true role with the *Spirit* sparked my interest in learning more. I began to ask my father an endless barrage of questions and to pore over family photographs and keepsakes. In the process, I learned more about the man my grandfather had been than I did about his role in changing the course of aviation history. A conservationist, backpacker, long-distance swimmer, paddleboarder, and prolific photographer, Donald Hall had a passion for the wilds of the world. He was a gentle man, most at home when sleeping under the stars and breathing the fresh mountain air.

He was also intrigued with flight and the machines that allowed man to touch the sky. My grandfather believed that through hard work, dedication, and an understanding of the forces around us, anything is possible. An inventor and an engineer, his attention was always focused on the next progressive leap in flight.

The more I learned about him, the more I came to admire my grandfather. Yet, his greatest and most well-known accomplishment, designing and building the *Spirit of St. Louis*, remained less real to me than who he had been as an individual. Soon that, too, would change.

In 1999, we were packing for a move to a smaller house south of Sedona. I was working in the garage, trying to decide what to keep, what to donate, and what to throw out. In the process of moving a stack of boxes, I uncovered a WWI-era steamer trunk with the initials D.A.H. on its side. Curious, I pried open the lid of the chest. The smell of old paper was immediate and intoxicating. As I rummaged through the contents, I found original manuscripts, drawings, film, photographs, and the original side drafts for the *Spirit of St. Louis*.

While this discovery amazed me, it reminded me of the many family keepsakes I had seen over the years. Had the special slide rule I had found in my grandfather's boxes been used in designing the *Spirit of St. Louis?* Had other items been hidden in front of us, waiting to be found for 75 years? I was eager to return to the research I had begun a few years earlier, again reviewing the letters, books, newspaper articles, photo negatives, and engineering equipment I had already found and, perhaps, misunderstood. But the steamer trunk was the missing link that would lead me to the truest of family treasures, that of discovering my heritage and my personal hero.

In researching my grandfather's life a few years earlier, many questions had formed in my mind. As I sorted through the contents of this historical treasure chest, they rose to the surface again. Why did the history Donald Hall helped create pass him by with little mention? Why did he finish his career with the Navy at North Island instead of at the head of his own Hall Aeronautical Company? What had Donald Hall thought as the aerospace industry left him behind? How did his brush with destiny change him, if it had changed him at all?

This book attempts to answer those questions as it chronicles the creation of the *Spirit of St. Louis* from the perspective of its designer and creator. In it you'll come to know Donald Hall not as a celebrity, but as an ordinary man who tapped into qualities inherent in all of us to achieve the extraordinary. It is my hope that reading SPIRIT & CREATOR will inspire you in the same way that coming to know my grandfather has inspired me. For his experience demonstrates that by applying ability, vision, hard work, integrity, and teamwork, an individual can change the course of history in as little as sixty days. ᔧ

— Nova Hall, GRANDSON

SPIRIT — THE CREATOR

N. A. Hall

THE MAN

"He was a gentle man,

most at home

when sleeping under

the stars

and breathing the

fresh mountain air...."

— NOVA HALL
Grandson, Donald A. Hall, Sr.

The Man

THERE WAS NOTHING PARTICULARLY REMARKABLE ABOUT HARLAN AND LOUISE HALL. New York natives and long-term residents of Brooklyn, the couple typified the working class American family. Harlan was employed by Western Union as a telegraph operator, while Louise cared for her husband, their home, and their three children. The couple's eldest son, Douglas, died while quite young. Daughter Alice was born in 1903 (she became Alice Hall-Smith when she married her first husband). Donald Albert Hall was their middle child.

Born December 7, 1898, Donald grew up in the era of Teddy Roosevelt's industrial revolution. It was a time of science and new inventions, and young Hall was fascinated by it all. His parents taught him to work hard and stressed the importance of a good education. They also instilled in him a strong sense of ethics, integrity, and justice.

As a result, Donald Hall grew to epitomize the characteristics of the responsible working man of the time, the same qualities that his father had embraced. He was honest, hardworking, fair, and devoted to his family and friends. Donald remained close to his parents and sister throughout his life, all of whom eventually relocated from Brooklyn to California after he established himself in San Diego.

Donald Hall was also a creative visionary with an artist's eye for beauty and a conservationist's passion for the natural world. Resourceful and energetic, he adopted a diverse collection of hobbies, most of them set in the great outdoors he loved. Among his activities were long-distance swimming, hiking, and canoeing. Perhaps it was growing up in the midst of a bustling city of concrete and steel that made the natural world so appealing to Hall. He was an early member of the Sierra Club and had a special fondness for the rock-tipped western mountains, the bleak deserts of Death Valley and Joshua Tree, and the ocean off the San Diego coastline.

Determined to protect the unspoiled wilderness, he became an avid environmentalist.

Hall was an accomplished photographer, as well, capturing on film whatever claimed his imagination. The wilderness, his family and friends, even work projects became targets for his camera's lens. Those photographs clearly demonstrate the breadth of his interests.

But despite his many abilities and activities, those who met him were most impressed by his uncompromising integrity, his unfailing humility, and a broad, welcoming smile. Donald Hall was a deeply modest and unassuming man. Those qualities did not, however, dampen his enthusiasm for technology or the spirit of invention and innovation with which he approached it. ⬎

. a .

. a . Donald A. Hall at three years of age.
. b . (inset photo) Donald A. Hall at 17, reading "Popular Mechanics." (1915).
. c . Portrait of Donald A. Hall (February, 1926).

(. a . - . c .) Provided by the estate of Donald A. Hall, Sr.

. c .

. d .

. e .

. f .

. d . & . e . Hall was an accomplished swimmer, winning several awards in long-distance swim meets. He found swimming relaxing and, at times, humorous.

. f . Although this photograph may look as if Hall enjoyed surfing, it's really a picture of Hall at the Santa Monica beach around 1925 with his paddleboard. Board surfing didn't catch on in Southern California until the 1950's.

(.d. - .f.) Provided by the estate of Donald A. Hall, Sr.

. h .

. g .

. j .

. i .

. g . Hall takes a break on a hike in Painted Canyon. He loved both the pine-covered mountains and the stark rock and sand of the desert.

. h . Hall at Big Bear Lake, California.

. i . Hall stands in front of a giant pine on a hiking trip in Southern California.

. j . Hall's personal Sierra Club directory.

(. g . - . j .) Provided by the estate of Donald A. Hall, Sr.

. l .

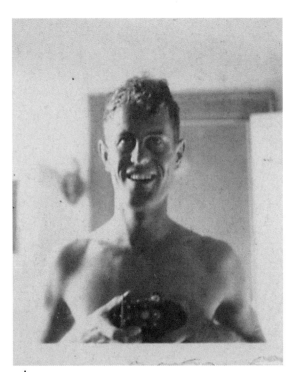

. k .

. m .

. o .

. k . Donald Hall was an accomplished photographer who sometimes enjoyed using his camera to joke around. This is Hall in a humorous self-portrait.

. l - . o . & . p . (opposite page) Fine examples of Hall's more serious approach to photography.

(. k . - . p .) Provided by the estate of Donald A. Hall, Sr.

. n .

Exposure 4 - 1/25 clear 7:45 AM

. q . Hall's efforts as an amateur photographer were rewarded when he won first prize in the Detroit News photo contest with an image of Eagle Point. The photo was taken in Yosemite Valley sometime after he joined the Douglas Company in Santa Monica in 1924. *Provided by the estate of Donald A. Hall, Sr.*

. r . . - u . A medley of images capturing Hall in his element. *Provided by the estate of Donald A. Hall, Sr.*

The Engineer

THE HEART OF BROOKLYN, NEW YORK, IN THE EARLY 1900'S WAS THE PERFECT ENVIRONMENT FOR A YOUNG BOY WITH DREAMS OF INVENTION AND INNOVATION. Progress was all around him. In 1902, the first air conditioner was invented. In 1904, New York's first subway opened, followed by the Manhattan Bridge in 1905. As buildings reached toward the sky, each was built taller than the last, pushing the engineering envelope. In an era of grand creations and impressive technological advances, much of it took place in New York City.

It was in this atmosphere that Donald Hall attended Manuel Training High School. In September of 1917, he was accepted into the prestigious Pratt Institute School of Science and Technology in Brooklyn. Oil tycoon and philanthropist Charles Pratt had founded the school in 1887 to teach the trades to its students. The school's motto, "Be True to Your Work and Your Work Will Be True to You," proved to be prophetic for Hall.

Originally planning a career in automotive design, Donald Hall enrolled in the School of Engineering with a focus in industrial mechanical engineering. He also joined the Student Army Training Corp (SATC), a precursor to the current ROTC. In 1919, he graduated from the Pratt Institute, earning a certificate in mechanical engineering.

In that same year, industrialist Raymond Orteig first offered a prize of $25,000 to any pilot who could cross the Atlantic non-stop from New York to Paris. Although the prize would one day change his life, the challenge had little significance to Hall at the time. He was focused on his new position as a junior draftsman at Curtiss Aeroplane & Motor Corp., the largest and most well-known American aircraft company of its day. Hall worked his way up in the company during the two years he spent there, becoming first a checker and then a designer. While working at Curtiss, he submitted a design that won a military award in 1921 for a night bombardment plane.

He was appointed acting chief engineer for Elias & Bros. that same year, and then went to work for L.W.F. Engineering Company in Long Island, New York. In 1924, Donald Hall relocated to Santa Monica to join the Douglas Company as an aerodynamics engineer. One of the fastest growing companies in the history of aviation, the Douglas Company provided Hall with valuable experience in designing long-range aircraft. Among his designs was a plane for the military that could fly from California to Honolulu. It was never built.

Hall took a leave of absence from Douglas in 1926 to become a pilot. No romantic notions or heroic fantasies prompted his application to the Army Air Corps. His motives were, instead, quite practical — Donald Hall wanted to learn about the aircraft he designed from the pilot's perspective. So, after passing the rigorous entrance exam, he became a cadet at Brooks Field in San Antonio, Texas.

His topography and land navigation manual bore the signature of a student from the previous class. Hall crossed out the name "C.A. Lindbergh" and signed his own. Little did he know that his path and that of Cadet Charles Lindbergh would soon cross again.

Only 5% of each training class graduated from the program. Although Donald Hall excelled in map reading, navigation, and other aviation skills, he didn't have the quick, intuitive reactions necessary to become a fighter pilot. He completed the course, but failed to make the final cut and, so, didn't earn his wings. Hall did, however, learn how to design an aircraft for the pilot, which was precisely what he had wanted to know.

He returned to his position at the Douglas Company with dreams of someday starting an aircraft design company of his own. In the meantime, he was offered an opportunity to work as a free-lance engineer for Ryan Airlines, a small aircraft manufacturing company that had approached Douglas for help. Hall was willing to drive the 260-mile round trip each weekend for a chance to work on some leading-edge designs.

Early in 1927, Benjamin Franklin Mahoney purchased his partner's portion of Ryan Airlines, Inc. He was looking for a talented aeronautical engineer with the experience to design a new aircraft model for the new company. Mahoney liked the hardworking young Hall and believed he had unique potential. So, on January 31, 1927, Donald Hall became the new chief engineer for Ryan Airlines. He was just 28 years old.

Three days later a telegram arrived from Robertson Aircraft Corp. in St. Louis. That message set in motion events that would soon change Donald Hall's future and the course of aviation history. ⤸

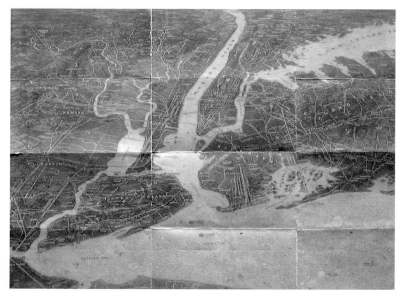

. a .

. b .

. c .

. a . A 1900's map of Brooklyn, Manhattan, and the surrounding boroughs of New York City.

. b . Hall began his career in 1919 as a junior draftsman for Curtiss Aircraft in New York. By the time he left Curtiss in 1921, he had been promoted to the position of designer.

. c . Donald A. Hall, the designer, at work.

. d . Airfoil model, inscribed with the date 1924.

(. a . - . d .) Provided by the estate of Donald A. Hall, Sr.

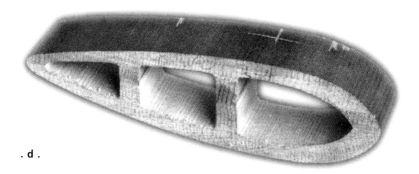

. d .

. e .

. f .

. h .

. e . Brooks Field Class of 1926. Hall is positioned in the second row from the top, eighth cadet in from the left.
. f . Cadet Donald A. Hall.
. g . (inset) Brooks Field barracks.
. h . Aerial view of Brooks Field, Austin, Texas.

(. e . - . h .) Provided by the estate of Donald A. Hall, Sr.

. i .

. i . Simulator flight training at Brooks Field.
. j . Structural design instruction at Brooks Field.
. k . A studious Cadet Hall in his barracks.
. l . This flight handbook for map reading and topography was one of Donald Hall's most prized possessions. When Hall received the handbook, he crossed out Lindbergh's name and signed his own. After the successful transatlantic flight, Hall added the "27" to commemorate the year the two men met.

(. i . - . l .) Provided by the estate of Donald A. Hall, Sr.

. j .

. k .

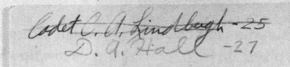

1. **Maps and mapping.**—AR 100–15, Maps and Mapping, states the basic principles underlying the classification, making, reproduction, issue, and use of standard and special maps. It assigns the making, procurement, supply, distribution, and reproduction of maps to the Corps of Engineers. It states the specifications governing standard maps, including the scale and title, and the type of map projection and quadrillage for use on all military maps of the United States.

2. **Scope.**—This pamphlet is the first of a series comprising the Training Regulations on Topography and Surveying. It states the *elementary* principles of map reading, including visibility and coordinates. Section VIII, Instruction Units, gives specific directions for performing the various operations which the average map reader must solve. Section IX, Training Course, comprises a series of typical jobs for training in map reading. More advanced principles of map reading are taken up in TR 190–15, Military Sketching, and TR 190–30, Use of Maps in Firing.

107639°—22——1

. l .

. m .

. n .

. m . &. n . Biplane models used at Brooks Field for pilot training.
. o . & . p . Flight maneuvers at Brooks Field.
. q . Cadet Hall in flight gear.
. r . (opposite page) Hall (far right) and fellow pilot candidates.

(. m . - . r .) Provided by the estate of Donald A. Hall, Sr.

. q .

. o .

. p .

SPIRIT — THE CREATION

WESTERN UNION

NEWCOMB CARLTON, PRESIDENT   J. C. WILLEVER, FIRST VICE-PR

The filing time as shown in the date line on full-rate telegrams and day letters, and the time of receipt at destination as sho

Received at 341 Plaza, San Diego, Calif. ALWAYS OPEN

SB149 14 6 EXTRA

WC LOSANGELES CALIF 21 828A

CAN YOU CONSTRUCT WHIRLWIND ENGINE PLANE

CAPABLE FLYING NONSTOP BETWEEN NEW YORK

AND PARIS STOP IF SO PLEASE STATE COST AND

DELIVERY DATE — ROBERTSON AIRCRAFT CORP

7M 3363   BY 855A RB

Concept

"It's increasingly obvious that the answer to my problem lies in Donald Hall, the engineer. My decision as to whether the Ryan Company is capable of building a plane with the performance I need must depend primarily on my estimate of him."

— CHARLES A. LINDBERGH
The Spirit of St. Louis (1953)

Concept

THE TELEGRAM SENT TO RYAN AIRLINES ON FEBRUARY 3, 1927, READ SIMPLY

CAN YOU CONSTRUCT WHIRLWIND ENGINE PLANE CAPABLE FLYING NONSTOP BETWEEN NEW YORK AND PARIS STOP IF SO PLEASE STATE COST AND DELIVERY DATE — ROBERTSON AIRCRAFT CORP.

Ryan Airlines initially responded that such an aircraft could be built within 90 days. When Lindbergh sent a second telegram requesting the plane in 60 days, Mahoney consulted chief engineer Donald Hall and then responded that Ryan Airlines could, indeed, meet the deadline. On February 23rd, Charles Lindbergh traveled to San Diego to determine for himself whether Ryan Airlines had the resources and ability to deliver the plane as promised. Lindbergh knew little about the small San Diego aircraft manufacturer that claimed it could custom-build a transatlantic airplane in two months. The team at Ryan airlines knew nothing of the young airmail pilot who intended to fly the plane until he walked through the factory doors.

When Lindbergh arrived at Ryan Airlines, chief engineer Donald Hall was the first to greet him. After a tour of the factory with owner B. F. Mahoney, Lindbergh met with Hall in the engineer's second-story office. Hall had made initial calculations before Lindbergh's arrival. Now they discussed the features the pilot had in mind while the young engineer created a preliminary sketch of the aircraft that was forming in his imagination.

Hall was surprised when he learned that Lindbergh intended to be the sole pilot on this long flight, but he soon realized that Lindbergh had carefully evaluated his options. He was determined to fly alone. The novel idea appealed to Hall, who recognized the logic of adding more fuel instead of another body. Still, he was

47

concerned about how Lindbergh would be able to stay awake and alert for an estimated forty-hour flight.

Both men were all too aware that pilots had already died attempting to cross the Atlantic. If this endeavor were to be successful, they would need to work very closely together and trust each other completely. Before meeting the engineer, Lindbergh had not been confident that the Ryan team could fulfill the 60-day deadline. After meeting Donald Hall, he was satisfied it could be done. This talented young engineer knew his trade. Lindbergh contacted his backers to finalize the agreement, and a contract was signed on February 25th.

They wasted no time, and work began three days later. Hall made room in his small office for another desk, as the tight time-frame required an almost continuous process of calculation, discussion, and recalculation. Lindbergh took a room at the YMCA where Hall was living to allow them to collaborate even when away from the manufacturing facility.

Lindbergh and Hall shared many qualities, including ingenuity, vision, and a passion for transforming ideas into reality. Both were educated and well read. This common ground created the basis for a growing friendship, as well as an effective working relationship. They knew that success would be largely dependent on Donald Hall's ability to design a plane that would fulfill the requirements of a long flight while maximizing Lindbergh's unique skills as a pilot. But, before the design phase could begin, several problems had to be solved. ✍

. a .

. c .

. d .

. a . Hardworking young Hall.

. b . Lindbergh at work on the trans-atlantic navigation charts and figures. The office he shared with Hall on the second floor of the Ryan manufacturing facility was quite small, but secure from outside distractions. They had set up a knocking system so they would not be disturbed.

. c . Ryan Airlines manufacturing facility.

. d . Ryan Airlines at Dutch Flats. *Courtesy of the San Diego Aerospace Museum.*

(. a . - . d .) Provided by the estate of Donald A. Hall, Sr.

. b .

. e .

. f .

. e . Lindbergh took a room at the YMCA where Hall was living to allow them to collaborate even when away from the manufacturing facility.

. f . Hall in his YMCA quarters.

. g . Hall photographed the view from his room at the YMCA.

(. e . - . g .) Provided by the estate of Donald A. Hall, Sr.

. g .

Planning

"After intensive preliminary design analyses of the aerodynamics, structures, and weights of various configurations of the proposed airplane, it was concluded that a redesign of the production model three-seater, open cockpit, Ryan M-2 could not make the 3,600 mile flight between New York and Paris with ample reserve fuel, and that a new design development was necessary."

— Donald A. Hall
The estate of Donald A. Hall, Sr.

Planning

The proposed airplane already had a name: the *Spirit of St. Louis.* But on February 25, 1927, it existed only in the mind of its designer. While Donald Hall knew it could be built in the specified time frame, he now had to prove it. Ryan Airlines used the best steel and manufacturing techniques available. However, this plane would be larger than normal and would put the skills of the Ryan crew to the test. He would be asking a lot of the men and women with whom he had only recently begun to work. Hall would be putting himself on the line, as well.

His calculations for aerodynamic flow, wing stress, and load would be key to the project, so Hall purchased a highly accurate engineer's slide rule, the best calculator he could find. As was his habit with every piece of equipment, Hall signed and dated the back of the instrument. Then he searched through books in his personal library and reviewed photographs from his work at Curtiss, Elias & Bros, and Douglas for ideas.

Many design issues came to mind. What type of landing gear would work best? What aerodynamic shape should he use? Which airfoil would be most effective? Before he made those decisions, however, he needed to know just how far the plane would fly as it crossed the Atlantic. Lindbergh had estimated a range of 3,500 miles, but Hall required a more exact number for his fuel calculations. Lacking a definitive source for the information, the pair drove to the nearest public library to find a globe. Using a piece of string, they measured a distance of 3,600 miles from New York to Paris. Rounding the figure to 4,000 provided a fuel reserve for potential navigational corrections. A flight of 4,000 miles would require four-hundred gallons of fuel.

For safety reasons, Lindbergh wanted the fuel tanks in front of the cockpit instead of behind it, the traditional position. In a crash landing the tanks could fly forward, crushing the pilot against the engine. Hall understood his reasoning, but was reluctant to comply, as the forward fuel tank would make it impossible for Lindbergh to see out the front of the plane. The pilot was confident he could fly on instruments alone and land by making shallow banks, using the limited view from the side windows to gauge his position. So, Hall relented, noting that the majority of fuel in this position would benefit the plane's center of gravity, thus its flight characteristics.

Lindbergh had insisted on a single Wright Whirlwind J-5C engine. Other planes attempting the transatlantic flight boasted Wright Whirlwinds, as well. However, Hall and Lindbergh believed that a single-engine design would be safer than a multi-engine plane. In addition, a single engine would result in a lighter total weight, decreasing fuel needs and increasing range. So, a single Wright Whirlwind was ordered, along with an Earth Inductor compass and a steel propeller.

Normally, a designer would do everything possible to make an aircraft stable. In this case, because the *Spirit's* wingspan would be increased and the fuselage expanded, optimum stability would require a larger tail surface. Besides, redesigning the tail surfaces would take time that Hall couldn't afford if the airplane were to be completed on schedule. Larger tail surfaces would decrease the plane's range, and the resulting stability would mean a greater likelihood that the pilot would fall asleep during a long flight. In flying a somewhat unstable plane, on the other hand, Lindbergh would have to keep his hand on the stick at all times. He was in favor of any feature that would help him remain awake as he crossed the Atlantic.

The Ryan M-2 tail surfaces and wing ribs would be incorporated into the final design, saving valuable time. However, Hall realized simple modifications to the Ryan M-2 or another existing Ryan model would not allow for a 4,000-mile flight, since 750% more fuel would be required. A completely new design was in order. ⌒

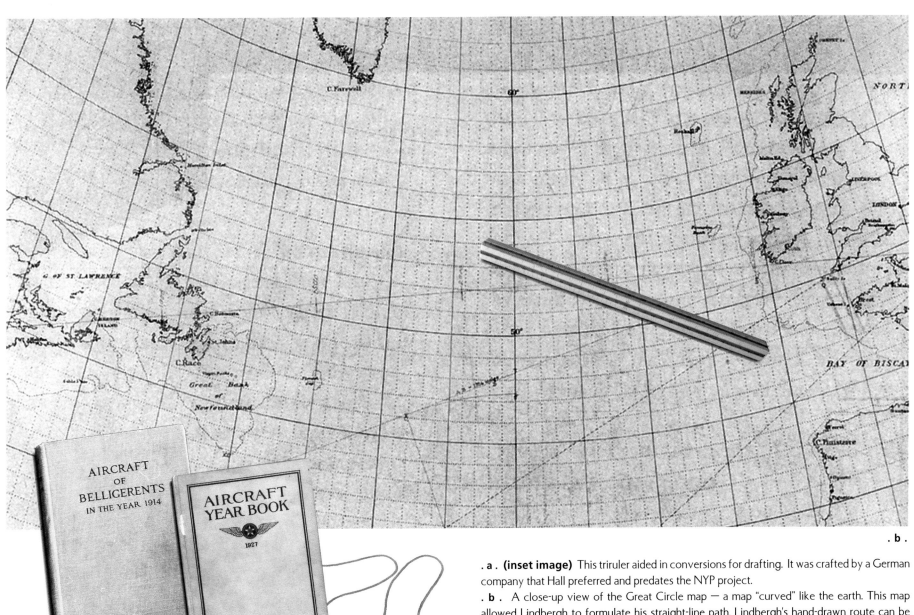

. b .

. a . (inset image) This triruler aided in conversions for drafting. It was crafted by a German company that Hall preferred and predates the NYP project.

. b . A close-up view of the Great Circle map — a map "curved" like the earth. This map allowed Lindbergh to formulate his straight-line path. Lindbergh's hand-drawn route can be seen, with 500-mile increments marked off.

. c . Two aeronautical books from Hall's extensive "pioneers of aviation" reference collection. Hall received "Aircraft of Belligerents" in 1919 while he was at the Pratt Institute.

(. a . - . c .) Provided by the estate of Donald A. Hall, Sr.

. c .

1

RYAN N.Y. TO PARIS AIRPLANE
MODEL N.Y.P.

DONALD A. HALL

GENERAL

Span — — — — — — — — — — — — —	46 ft.
Chord — — — — — — — — — — — —	7 ft.
Wing Area — — — — — — — — — —	319 sq.ft.
Aerofoil — — — — — — — — — . —	Clark Y
Engine — —Wright J-5-C giving 223 B.H.P. at 1800 R.P.M.
Propeller — — Standard Steel Propeller Co. -dural. set at 16¼° pitch

WEIGHTS

Empty complete with instruments — . — — — 2150 lbs.

Useful Load

Pilot — — — — — — — — — — — —	170
Miscellaneous — — — — — — — — — —	40
Gasoline - 425 gal. (Western at 6.12 lbs. per gal.) — —	2600
Oil — 25 gal. at 7 lbs. per gal. — — — — —	175
	2985 lbs

Gross weight fully loaded at start of flight - - 5130 lbs.
" " lightly " " end " " without gasoline.
and food but with 10 gal. oil left — — — 2415 lbs.

LOADING

Wing Loading {Full Load at start of flight = 16.1 lbs./sq.ft
              {Light Load at end " " = 7.57 "

Power Loading {Full Load at start of flight = 23.0 lbs./B.H.P.
               {Light Load at end " " = 10.8 "

CALCULATED PERFORMANCE (R.P.M. data based on test and theory)

Maximum Speed {Full Load = 120 M.P.H
               {Light Load = 124.5 M.P.H

Minimum Speed {Full Load = 71 M.P.H
               {Light Load = 49 M.P.H.

Economic Speed {Full Load = 97 M.P.H. at 1670 R.P.M.
                {Light Load = 67 M.P.H. at 1080 R.P.M.

By D. Hall 5-9-27

2

RYAN N.Y.P. AIRPLANE

Fuel Economy at Economic Speeds

Full Load with full rich mixture = 6.95 miles per gallon
Light Load with lean mixture = 13.9 " " " "

Range

At ideal speeds of 97 start and 67 M.P.H at end = 4110 miles
At practical " 95 " " 75 " " " = 4040 "

FLIGHT TEST PERFORMANCE

Maximum Speed

With 25 gal. gas and 5 gal. oil = 129 M.P.H. over 3 K.M. course
" full load of 425 gal. gas and 25 gal. oil = 124 M.P.H.
approximate based on calculated performance.
With 25 gal. gas and 4 gal. oil by air speed meter = 128 M.P.H.
" 201 " " " " " " = 127 " "

Take Off Distances

Tests made at Camp Kearney near San Diego, Calif
at 600 ft. altitude. Oil = 4 gallons.

Gallons Gas	Gross Wt.	Approx. Head Wind Vel.	Take Off Dist. FT.
36 — — —	2600 lbs — —	7 M.P.H. —	229 ft.
71 — —	2800 — —	9 —	287
111 — —	3050 — —	9 —	389
151 — —	3300 — —	6 —	483
201 — —	3600 — —	4 —	615
251 — —	3900 — —	2 —	800
301 — —	4200 — —	0 — —	1023

RYAN AIRLINES
Donald A. Hall, Chief Engineer and Designer
Donald A. Hall
SAN DIEGO, CALIF.
MAY. 9, 1927

. d .   . e .

. d . & . e . A May 9, 1927, redraft of chief engineer Hall's preliminary design and load calculations. *Provided by the estate of Donald A. Hall, Sr.*

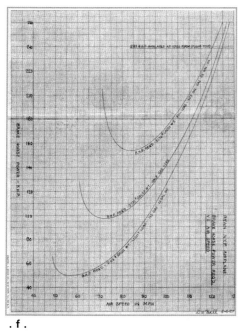

. f .

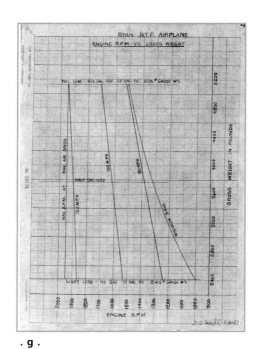

. g .

. f .   Curves of h.p. required versus airspeed for full load, half load, and light.

. g .   Engine R.P.M. versus gross weight.

. h .   Engine R.P.M. versus airspeed at various gross weights.

. i .   Miles per pound of gas versus airspeed.

. j .   Airspeed and R.P.M. versus distance.

(. f . -. j .) May 4-7, 1927, redrafts of chief engineer Hall's preliminary calculations, provided by the estate of Donald A. Hall, Sr.

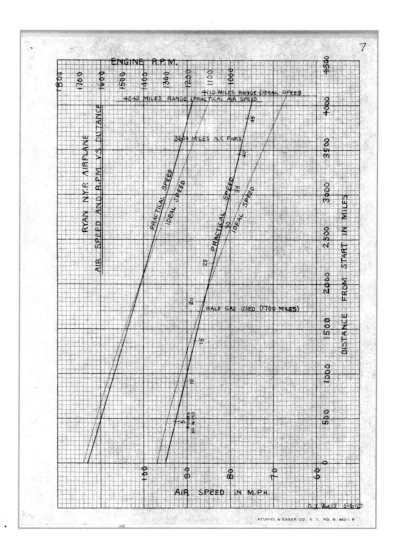

. h .

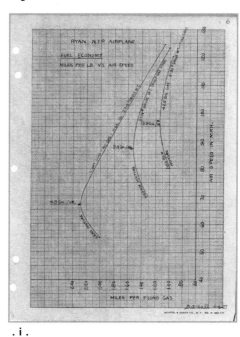

. i .

. j .

57

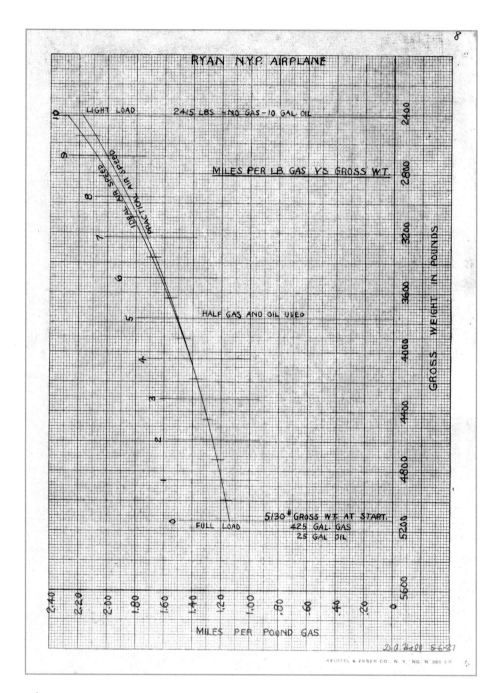

. k .

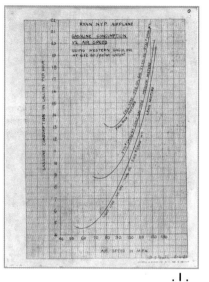

. l .

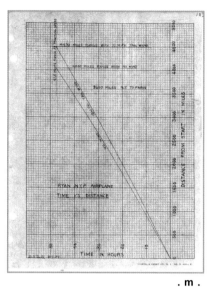

. m .

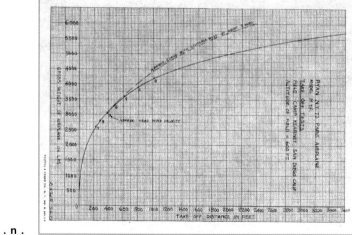

. n .

. k .   Miles per pound of gas versus gross weight.
. l .   Gas consumption versus airspeed.
. m .   Time versus distance for no wind and for a following wind of 10 m.p.h.
. n .   Results of take-off tests at Camp Kearney (600 ft. above sea level).

(. k . - . n .) May 4-7, 1927, redrafts of chief engineer Hall's preliminary calculations, provided by the estate of Donald A. Hall, Sr.

Design

"Pencil lines curve
and angle delicately
over the face of
his drafting board's
white sheet. A fuselage
is taking outline form.
He's been sitting on that
stool since early morning,
with no break . . .
It was the same yesterday,
and the day before."

— CHARLES A. LINDBERGH
The Spirit of St. Louis (1953)

Design

MOST PLANES ARE IN THE DESIGN PROCESS FOR YEARS BEFORE THEY GO INTO PRODUCTION. With a 60-day deadline, that was not a luxury Hall could afford in designing the *Spirit of St. Louis.* All other projects were put on hold so that he could focus his full attention on the *Spirit.*

While Hall began the design, Lindbergh taught himself to fly by the stars and by instrument. As an airmail pilot, he had become proficient in flying blind through storms, fog, and other forms of inclement weather. He was also an expert at dead reckoning, navigating by sighting roads, rivers, and other ground references. Over the ocean, this would not be possible. It would be a flight unlike anything the young pilot had ever experienced. Lindbergh had flown mainly biplanes in the Army Reserves and throughout his airmail career. While the *Spirit's* design progressed, he learned the new characteristics of high-wing monoplanes through flight performance tests in the Ryan M-1, gaining valuable experience flying this new breed of aircraft.

At Ryan, the production team, headed by manager Hawley Bowlus, waited as Hall began the design process. The chief engineer had to carefully coordinate his design work with the manufacturing schedule. Hall knew that valuable time would be wasted if the production crew were idle while waiting for him to develop a complete set of plans. Instead, he produced the designs for each individual component, planning the sequence so that the parts could be built in the most effective order. However, accomplishing that required that he quickly create a preliminary overall design. There was no space for error and no time to rebuild an ill-conceived component.

Initially, Hall set the crew to work on finishing the frame. The fuselage frame needed to be approximately thirty inches longer than any previous Ryan model. The framework was of an entirely new design that Hall had already begun. It was under construction prior to Lindbergh's arrival in San Diego. The huge main fuel tank needed to match this pre-existing frame and thus was designed for a custom fit. The center of gravity (CG), crucial for an aircraft's performance, would be enhanced by the placement of the fuel tanks under the wing and near the theoretical CG. However, preserving this calculated balance with the engine's substantial weight would require extending the nose by two feet.

The wing required special attention, as well. Using a spare piece of cardboard, Hall hand sketched the initial wing design so the wing department could start work immediately. To increase fuel efficiency and load capacity, the length was to be extended by ten feet. Later, Hall would use this sketch to create one of the few blueprints produced during the sixty-day construction of the *Spirit*. The blueprint specified the size and spacing of each rib, as well as the structural modifications necessary for the additional length of the wing. The Clark "Y" airfoil was selected to maximize performance and achieve the minimum 10 mpg efficiency the *Spirit* needed to succeed.

The next design component to be completed involved the fuel tanks, followed by the landing gear. Due to the massive weight caused by the large fuel capacity, Hall chose a landing gear design that had proven successful in German aircraft. It would be strong enough to handle the special stresses this plane would experience.

Hall designed the cockpit to Lindbergh's unusual specifications. The pilot wanted an Earth Inductor compass, but no radio. The traditional pedals for the rudder control would be included, along with an oak-handled lever on the left for stabilizer trim. The throttle control was located just below and behind it. The pilot's seat was to be a wicker chair specially made to Lindbergh's proportions.

The main fuel tank, positioned in front of the cockpit, eliminated the traditional forward window, but two side windows would be included. There would be no parachute on this flight. In designing the cockpit, reducing weight was a primary goal, so anything that wasn't essential was omitted.

Hall was in a race against time. Everyone at the factory was aware that other pilots and other planes were preparing for the same flight across the Atlantic. Lindbergh desperately wanted to make his attempt before any of them succeeded. The young chief engineer worked tirelessly, week after week, at one point staying on task for 36 hours straight without sleep. He eventually logged 775 engineering hours on the *Spirit's* design. ⬟

. a . Hall, working day and night, would average 86 hours per week in sixty days.

. b . Pictured are some of the drafting tools that Donald Hall and Charles Lindbergh used on the NYP project. Lindbergh borrowed some of Hall's equipment to make calculations and produce his navigational maps. The case that held the prized equipment is badly deteriorated and three compasses are missing. One compass is on display at Lindbergh Field in San Diego.

. c . In the process of designing the *Sprit,* Donald Hall did not have time to create actual aircraft blueprints. These two images are part of the mechanical "blue print" engineering calculations Hall needed for the redesigned wing. (left) Shows a wing spar, specifying how wide and high the ribs should be. To save time, the ribs for the M-1 were determined to be useful and were incorporated into the final design. (right) Shows the internal cross supports which were necessary for determining structural integrity in the lengthened wing components.

. d . Hall's special slide rule was larger than the standard slide rule. This precision instrument allowed him to make the exact calculations necessary for building the "perfect" airplane. Approximately twenty-four inches long, it was made of mahogany. Donald A. Hall signed and dated it 1927.

(. a . - . d .) Provided by the estate of Donald A. Hall, Sr.

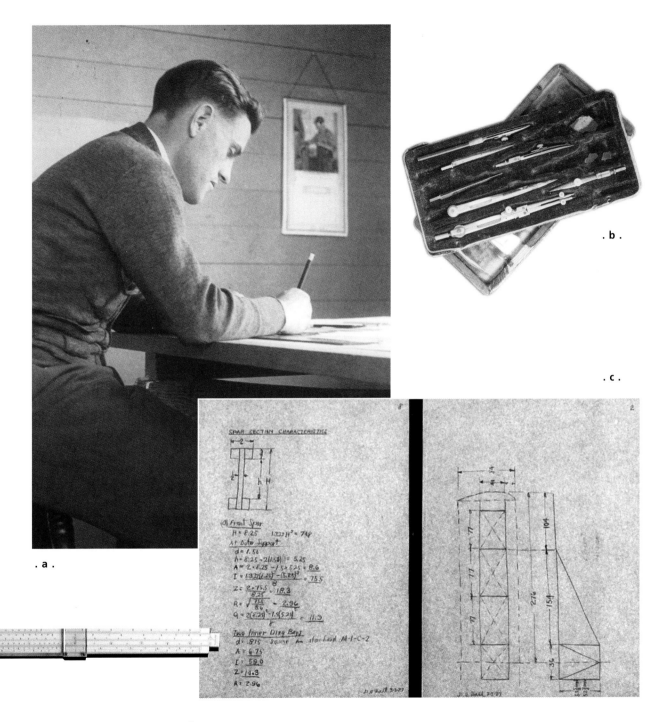

. b .

. c .

. a .

. d .

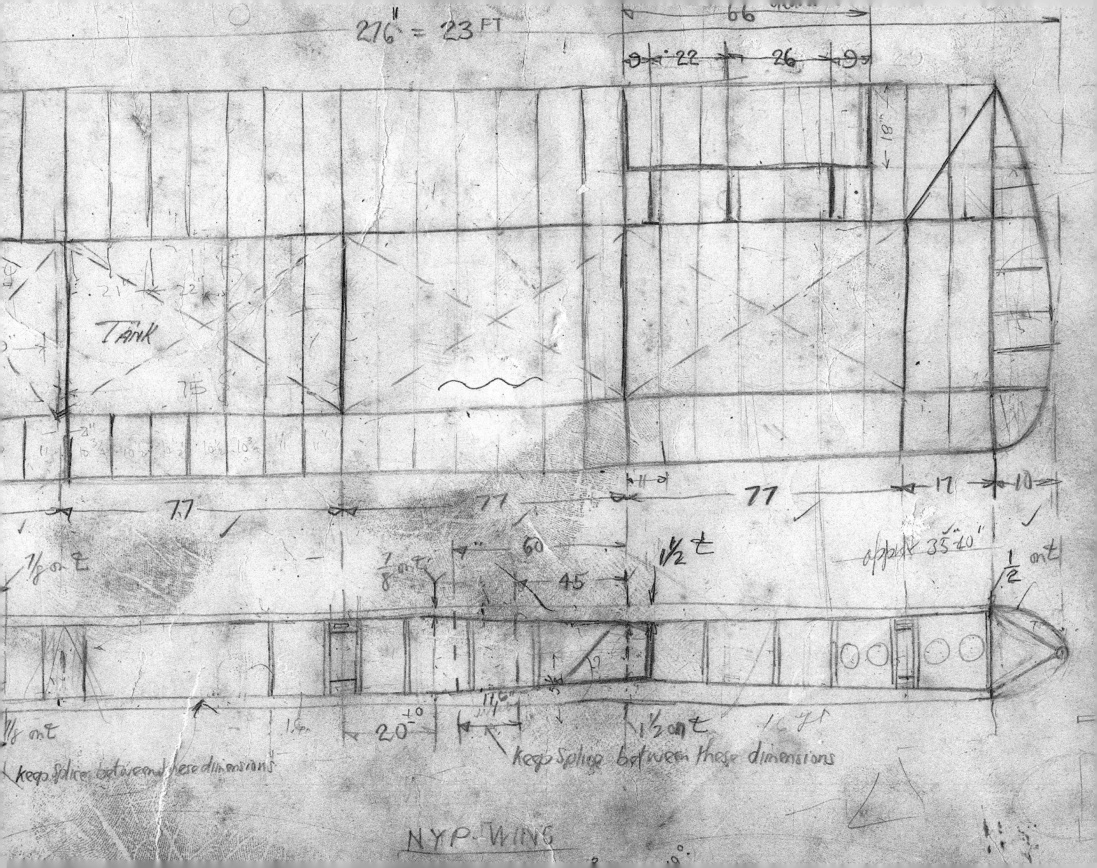

NYP WING

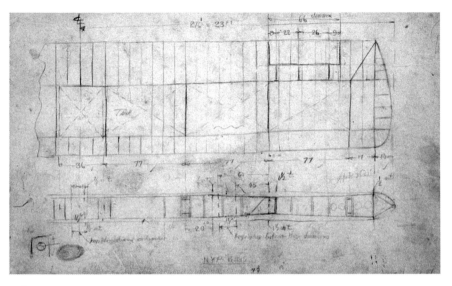

. f .

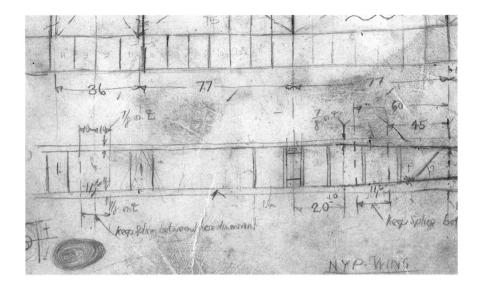

. g .

. h .

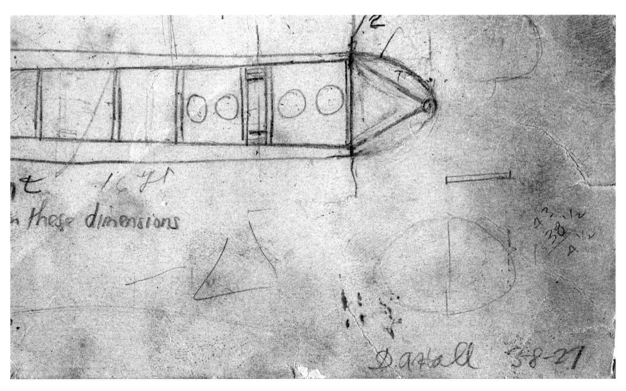

. e . (opposite page) & . f . - . h . This early hand-sketched drawing was the working model for the *Spirit's* wing. Hall had to extend the wing by 10 feet, requiring many calculations to maintain the wing's structural integrity. Hall also had to design the wing tips so they would be aerodynamic with the least drag, an extra step most designs of the time skipped. The purpose was to add fuel economy, and, thus, enhance range. This sketch survived the 60 days and remained in Hall's collection for over 70 years. His signature is barely visible in the lower right corner. *Courtesy of the Karpeles Museum.*

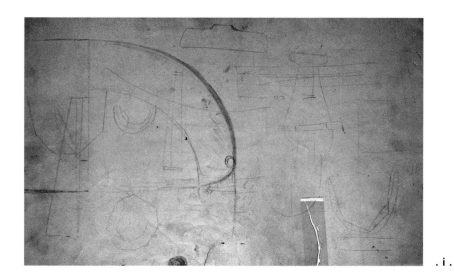

. i . This image shows the backside of Hall's hand-drawn sketch of the *Spirit's* wing. Donald Hall's fingerprints are perfectly and permanently saved on the front and back of this amazing piece of history.

. j . This image depicts the side view and half of the top down view (at top) of the *Spirit* fuselage. The linen drawing shows the calculations Hall made to determine the curvature of the nose section, thus achieving the *Spirit's* peak aerodynamic shape for economical flight. The design illustrated the optimal efficiency in flight that was of prime importance to Hall and Lindbergh.

(. i . and . j .) Provided by the estate of Donald A. Hall, Sr.

. i .

. j .

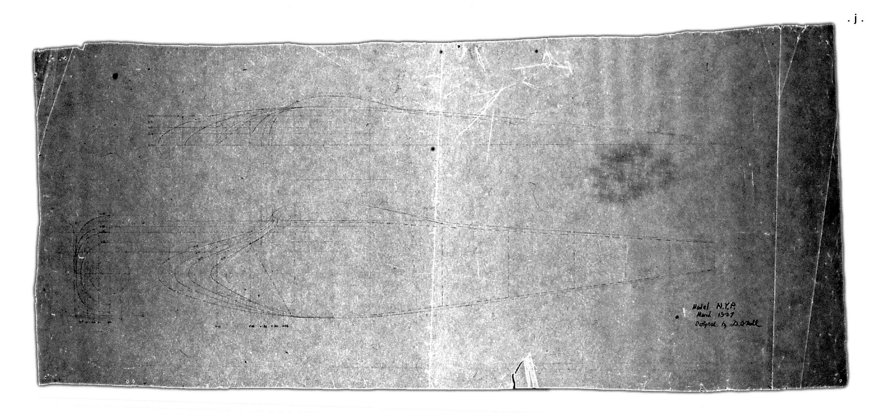

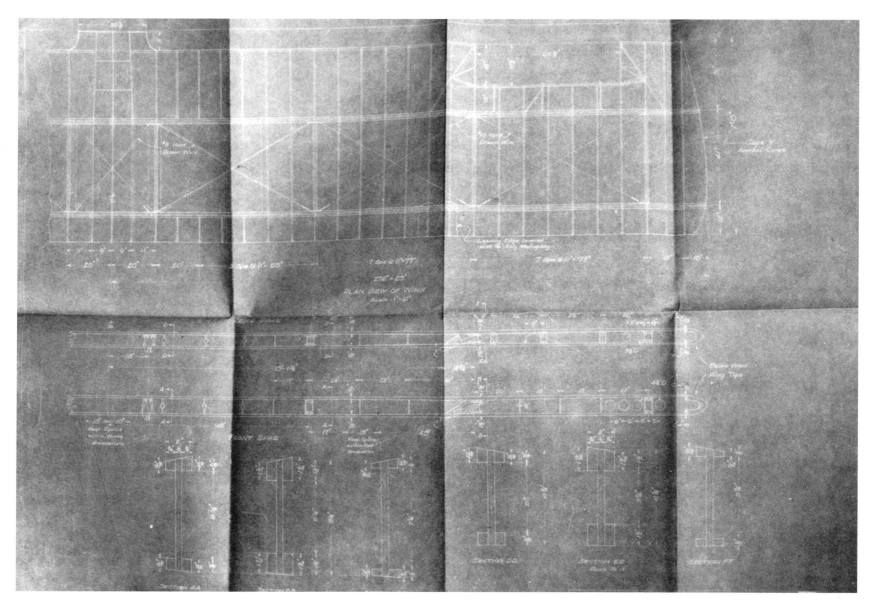

. k . There was no time to produce authentic blueprints during the initial NYP (New York to Paris) project. These blueprints were made for the NYP-2, an aircraft identical to the *Spirit* that was sold to the Japanese and later destroyed. Pictured is an NYP-2 blueprint of the wing and spar based on the original hand-sketched shop drawing of the *Spirit*. From top to bottom: (1) A top down view of the wing showing spar placement and spacing, aileron placement, and other structural/design elements. (2) The various "spars," which created and maintained the Clark "Y" airfoil shape along the entire wing surface. *Provided by the estate of Donald A. Hall, Sr.*

. l .

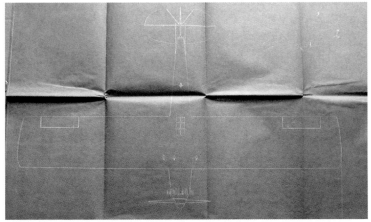

. m .

. n.

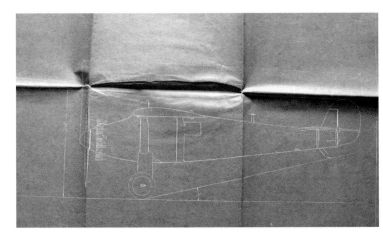

. o .

. l . - . o . Pictured from the NYP-2 blueprints, these images depict front, side, and top views of the *Spirit*. *Provided by the estate of Donald A. Hall, Sr.*

	1927			RYAN AIRLINES			

WEEK OF	MODEL	PART OF AIRPLANE	TYPE OF WORK		TIME - HOURS	
					JOB	WEEK
(Monday) Jan 31	M-1-C-2	Wings	Stress Analysis		47	47
Feb 7	M-1-C-2	"	" "		22	} 54
" 7	M-1-B-2	Airplane	" "		32	
" 14	M-1-B-2	"	" "		32	} 48
14	M-1-C-2	Wings	" "		16	
21	M-1-C-2	"	" "		16	}
" 23 & 24	M-1-B-2	Chassis	" "		16	} 54
" 25-27	N.Y.P.	Airplane	Entire Design incl. dwgs.		22	
28	N.Y.P.	"	"		60	60
Mar. 7	N.Y.P.	"	"		66	66
14	N.Y.P.	"	"		72	72
21	"	"	"		73	73
28	"	"	"		74	74
April 4	"	"	"		79	79
11	"	"	Total = 36½ (not 32) hours Worked from 5.45 A.M. Monday to 6.15 P.M. Tuesday without sleep		67	67
18	"	"	"		81	81
24	"	"	"		74	74
May 2	"	Performance Tests	Performance calcul. & test & photo (Worked from 7.45AM Thursday to 11:30AM Friday = 26 hours time)		84	84
"	"	"	Monday		14	
			Total time on N.Y.P.		768	
			" " performance test =		98	

Production

> "The presence of
> Charles Lindbergh,
> with his keen
> knowledge of flying,
> his understanding
> of engineering problems,
> his implicit faith
> in the proposed flight
> ...was a most important factor
> in welding together
> the entire factory organization
> into one smoothly
> running team."
>
> — DONALD A. HALL
> *The estate of Donald A. Hall, Sr.*

MEMBERS OF THE
RYAN AIRLINES FACTORY ORGANIZATION
RESPONSIBLE FOR THE CONSTRUCTION OF
THE SPIRIT OF ST. LOUIS:

Mr. B.F. Mahoney, President of Ryan Airlines
Mr. W.H. Bowlus, Factory Manager
Donald A. Hall, Chief Design Engineer
Mr. Bert Tindale, Shop Superintendent & Wing Dept.
Mr. Walter Locke, Purchasing Dept. & Egn. Ast.
Mr. McNeal, Final Assembly Dept.
Mr. Fred Rohr, Tank & Cowling Dept.
Mr. Fred Ayers, Covering & Finishing Dept.
Mr. Anderson, Welding Dept.
Mr. Morrow, Fitting Dept.

— Technical Notes National Advisory Committee for Aeronautics,
No. 257, "Technical Preparation of the Airplane
SPIRIT OF ST. LOUIS" written for the
National Advisory Committee for Aeronautics
by Donald A. Hall, Chief Engineer, Ryan Airlines, Inc.,
Washington, July 1927

Production

DESIGN AND PRODUCTION PROGRESSED IN TANDEM. As soon as Donald Hall completed the design for each component, the production crew swung into action to build it as quickly and efficiently as possible. They worked under the supervision of production manager Hawley Bowlus and the watchful eye of Charles Lindbergh. Although the pilot's quiet observation initially unnerved the crew, they soon grew accustomed to his frequent presence.

The lower level of the facility housed the fittings and fuselage departments, along with the main business office, stock room, and sheet metal department. Upstairs, spanning the front of the building, were the engineering office, wood shop, and wing assembly section. A monorail system moved the wings along the production line from fabric covering to doping to finishing. The *Spirit's* fuselage was the first component to be completed. As other fuselage components were finished, they, too, were installed into the large frame.

The tubular steel frame that would support the entire structure was welded together and treated to prevent oxidation. The main fuselage fuel tank, one of five hand-built tanks, was designed to hold 210 gallons of fuel. Once it was installed through the top of the frame, the unfinished wing was briefly attached to the fuselage above the tank, confirming its correct fit.

When it was determined that more workers were needed, several Ryan employees were transferred to metalworking and welding from other departments. With few jigs or guides available for the custom-designed parts, production was a painstaking and demanding process. Many crew members voluntarily worked long hours of overtime. A few offered ideas, as well. Albert Clyde Randolph, who worked in the wing rib department, was one of them. He came up with the idea of a periscope to provide Lindbergh with a forward view. After Hall verified that a periscope wouldn't hinder the *Spirit* aerodynamically, it was added to the cockpit.

The tail section began to take a classic shape as the rudder and elevators were added. The tail stabilizers were constructed from wielded steel tubing and later fabric covered. The controls were actuated, allowing Lindbergh to control the *Spirit* via a traditional cable and pulley system. The tailskid, which jutted out from under the end of the tail section, was used for braking and directional control. A bungee system was used to absorb the shock of the rough fields of the day.

The fuselage was placed against a brick wall in front of a white panel so that Hall could photograph the main fuel tank, cockpit, and tail section. Hall doubled as the parts inspector as each component was finished. Arriving at the facility hours before the work crews, he would check that each part was built to his and Lindbergh's specifications. As the fuselage took its final shape, the front nose section was removed so that the oil tank and 88-gallon forward fuel tank could be installed. Once finished, the Wright Whirlwind engine could be installed, as well. The 25-gallon oil tank rested directly behind the engine and in front of the forward fuel tank.

The wing was built up with wooden reinforced "I" section spars. The wing ribs were built-up from square wooden sticks and held together with glue gussets, a common design for the time. Production on the wing took a great deal of time, but could not be rushed. It was uniquely designed with the addition of an airfoil-shaped wing tip to minimize drag. Built from strips of balsa wood and covered in cloth, the tips gave the *Spirit's* wing an unusual teardrop shape, ideal for a long oceanic flight.

The ailerons were smaller than those of the Ryan M-2. Made of steel and covered with fabric, they reduced wing tip deflection and increased aerodynamic efficiency during the long flight over the ocean, but lateral stability suffered at low speeds. As the wing's production neared completion, the three wing fuel tanks were installed. The center tank would hold 36 gallons of fuel, while those balanced on the right and left would each hold 58 gallons, further benefiting the plane's center of gravity.

The landing gear, designed for the *Spirit's* heavy takeoff weight, required special shocks created from heat-treated steel and multiple heavy-duty shock cords. The wheels were attached to the axle portion of the lower Y-shaped struts, whish was, in turn, attached to the shock and fuselage. The result was a well-balanced, exceptionally tough, and structurally sound landing gear with an especially wide tread.

The *Spirit of St. Louis* was almost complete. Final assembly was scheduled for April 27, the last day before the *Spirit's* initial test flight would take place. ⌒

. a . (top left) The frame, which was custom built for Lindbergh, was the first component the Ryan team worked on. Once finished, the tailskid would make it difficult to move the aircraft, so handles were welded to the tail portion of the frame.

(top right) This image shows the area (at center) where the main gas tank would be installed. The cockpit is to the left, marked by the shiny silver control stick. Once the main gas tank was installed, the field of vision became virtually zero since the forward view was completely blocked. The blackened points at the top right joints reveal recent welding.

(bottom right) The *Spirit* was both a piece of engineering mastery and a piece of art (its form followed its function). To accommodate the intense structural stress that 425 gallons of fuel would place on the frame, additional steel tubing was used. Notice the extensive use of the triangle throughout the design for added strength. The circle at the front of the frame is the engine mounting ring.

Provided by the estate of Donald A. Hall, Sr.

. b . (top left) The tubing used in building the *Spirit* was high quality, 1020 mild-carbon steel, specially treated inside and out at Ryan to protect the ocean-flying plane from corrosion.

(top right) On the underside of the frame, where the first sawhorse meets the framework, an "extra" joining point is used for strengthening the main fuel compartment with additional steel tubing. This technique also allowed the transfer of force from the lower fuselage to the upper fuselage. Notice that the newly added nose section appears darker than the already primed body section, indicating it was recently finished and attached.

(bottom left) Even at this early stage, the *Spirit's* final form was taking shape. In this photo, the darker tubing outlines the nose section, which Hall had determined needed to be extended by 18 inches. Notice the darker rudder pedals just behind the main tank compartment on the lower section.

Provided by the estate of Donald A. Hall, Sr.

. c . Once covered and installed, this 210-gallon tank, made from ternplate (a soft tin-steel), would hold the majority of the fuel Lindbergh would use in his flight to Paris. The "baffles" and grid-like structure helped limit the fuel from sloshing inside the tank. Hand-crafted to fit perfectly in the front of the cockpit, the main fuel tank was much larger than anything the workers had built before.

Although this placement would block Lindbergh's forward view, it would increase the pilot's safety in the event of a crash landing. The forward inertia would send the tank and fuel into the engine without crushing the pilot.

Few of the Ryan workers initially knew the purpose of the huge tank, as secrecy was maintained about many details of the project. No matter what its intended use, the tank had to be perfect since a single leak could make the difference between success and tragedy.

(top center) The tank is resting on its front, with the top section toward Hall as he took the photo.

(right) Notice the tiny pre-drilled holes along the edges for the rivets that would firmly attach the ternplate covering to the fuel tank. Once riveted, the seams were soldered to make it leak proof.

Provided by the estate of Donald A. Hall, Sr.

. d . Once the frame and main fuel tank were finished, the two pieces were joined by "dropping" the tank into the mid-section of the frame from above. Though not completely finished, this image shows how the frame, the main fuel tank, and wing struts are attached. Notice the tiny triangular wooden sawhorses holding up the entire assembly. *Provided by the estate of Donald A. Hall, Sr.*

. e . **(top left)** In this close-up, you see the wires and fuel lines leading past the main fuel tank. The triangular-shaped piece with multiple holes drilled in it allowed the pilot to fine-tune the trim settings for difficult flight conditions. The production crew was installing the fuel and oil lines using single long metal tubes when Lindbergh caught this potentially fatal problem. Instead, the tubes were cut in 18 inch (or shorter) lengths, then connected with clamps to prevent possible engine failure due to vibration, which had stressed and broken long metal tubes in other planes Lindbergh had piloted.

(top right) In this image, the nose section of the frame is missing. It would be reattached later with the Whirlwind engine. Notice the pre-wiring, fuel tubing, and straps holding the main fuel tank in place.

(bottom right) Here, the thin wood instrument panel, control stick, and left window frame are visible. Attached to the small triangular piece in the center of the photo is the trim lever with its laminated wooden handle. Just behind and below is the throttle lever (with a round laminated handle) that would allow Lindbergh to set the engine RPM and the plane speed, thus controlling fuel economy.

Provided by the estate of Donald A. Hall, Sr.

. f . **(opposite page)** The *Spirit's* instrument panel changed many times before its final design. This image shows one of the initial set-ups. The fuel control system is visible at the bottom of the image. On the far right side of the instrument panel there is a new addition, a clear vertical tube that Lindbergh invented. This "Econometer" was created to help Lindbergh monitor fuel consumption on his flight across the Atlantic. Because it didn't function properly, it was removed once he arrived in New York City from San Diego.

. g .

. h .

. i .

. g . In this view from inside the *Spirit's* frame, the left rudder pedal well and the base of the fuel system/filter are visible. Notice the shiny silver control stick at the lower left of the photo. The throttle lever is out of view (off to the left). The small metal piece connected to a black circular shape, with two fuel lines leading into it, is the "wobble pump." This pump allowed Lindbergh to move fuel from the lower tanks to any of the wing tanks, which allowed fuel to be gravity fed into the engine if the engine pump failed. As a safety device, if something critical had occurred in the fuel system, Lindbergh could have pumped his way to France.

. h . This view shows the left side of the cockpit from a vantage outside the frame. The control stick in the center of the image is angled towards the viewer. To the right is the future location of the wicker chair. The throttle lever, with its ball-shaped handle, is clearly visible in the "off" position. The fuel valves are on the left side of the image in the background (out of focus). Notice the newly added doorframe in the background.

. i . **(top center)** This, the final photo in the cockpit series, shows all the controls Lindbergh would utilize while on his historic flight. Visible are the still-changing instrument panel, the fuel system below it, the trim lever **(inset)**, the throttle lever, the tiny wobble pump, the pedals to control the rudder, and the control stick leaning off to the right. The instrument panel was made of plywood, with the gauges from various manufacturers set into the elliptically cut wood. Later, Hall would take one final photograph of the finished "San Diego version" instrument panel.

(. f . - . i .) Provided by the estate of Donald A. Hall, Sr.

. j .

. j . The large cylindrical generator for the earth inductor compass, which Lindbergh required as part of the design, is visible in the center of this tail section photo. A thin rod extending from the back of the fuselage was attached to the generator. Four anemometer type cups would spin the shaft as air traveled over the plane, generating the electrical current needed for this newly invented navigational tool. Once the course was set into the compass controller, the pilot would simply maintain his course according to the gauge in the panel. It was necessary, however, to correct for deviation/wind speed and reset the course every 100 miles (once per hour). The tailskid, which is holding up the tail section, can be seen at the far right.

. k . This photo provides a close-up view of the tailskid. The tailskid worked to slow the aircraft down as the aircraft had no brakes. The bungee was to absorb the shock from the rough fields of the day. Because it would have to endure extreme structural stress, the tailskid itself was constructed of special steel that had been heat-treated to 180,000 psi. A removable panel allowed access to the tailskid assembly for maintenance.

. l . When the metal tailskid rod contacted the ground, force was applied upwards toward the fuselage. At the same time, the tip of the tailskid rod inside the fuselage, which was attached to the "bungee" cord would pull down against the cord. The elastic bungee acted as a shock while the whole assembly allowed directional control and braking. This type of tailskid was ideal for both the mud-packed surface of New York's airfield and the grass airfield at Le Bourget.

(. j . - . l .) Provided by the estate of Donald A. Hall, Sr.

. k .

. l .

. m . This image highlights the vertical stabilizer (fin) and tailskid in the lower right corner of the picture. Although many components had been installed at this point, several remained to be finished before the aircraft was covered with fabric. The base of the tailskid is flat shaped, which emphasizes its purpose to "run" along the airfield surface. The metal tip at the base of the tail is useful in case of a hard landing. *Provided by the estate of Donald A. Hall, Sr.*

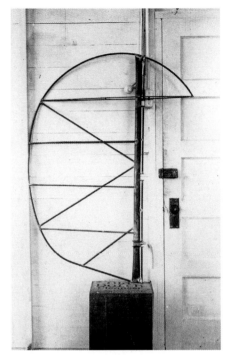

. n .

. o .

. p .

. n . and . o . Although the *Spirit* needed larger tail surfaces, there was insufficient time to custom-design them. Lindbergh and Hall made the decision that a slightly unstable plane, utilizing the too-small tail surfaces of the Ryan M-2, would be good enough. They agreed that the instability might even help Lindbergh stay awake for the estimated 40 hours to Paris. The tail surfaces used in the *Spirit* included: **(.n.)** the rudder, which governed yaw control, and **(.o.)** the elevator, which allowed the pilot to select the angle of attack for more or less lift while giving pitch control in flight.

. p . This image shows the non-movable section of the horizontal stabilizer. The two wood spacers at the top left of the photo allowed the M-2 parts to function and fit properly on the newly designed airframe.

(. n . - . p .) Provided by the estate of Donald A. Hall, Sr.

84

. q . **(right)** Painstakingly hand built, the wing used the Clark "Y" airfoil, an efficient and commonly used design. This choice also incorporated the existing M-2 wing "rib" design, thus saving time. However, the wing had to be extended ten feet in length to handle the increased load. The vertical ribs are placed at exact distances for the wing's structural strength and airfoil shape. The "leading edge" of the wing, which appears at the bottom of the image, is covered with plywood. At the right corner of the photo, notice the circular pulley next to the Ryan worker's shoe. The cable leading back along the wing to the cockpit from the pulleys allowed the pilot to control the ailerons and thus all roll movements. The left and right wing fuel tanks will be installed later in the two rectangular holes that are visible in the wing.

(bottom right) This image shows the left tip of the wing with a large gap in its trailing edge for the ailerons (which were installed at a later point). The custom-designed and specially built wing tip was already attached. Not all the "ribs" were the same. Certain ribs at pre-determined measurements were reinforced for added strength. It was at these reinforced ribs that the drag wires were anchored. Notice the ribs hanging on the wall, ready to be used depending on the size and need. The Ryan manufacturing plant was designed to be highly efficient, so that no time would be wasted.

Provided by the estate of Donald A. Hall, Sr.

. q .

. r . In this photo the wing is upside down so the tip can be finished with additional strips of balsa wood. The underside of the aerodynamic wing tip is more curved while the upper side is flatter. This view is from the trailing edge of the wing toward the leading edge. The unfinished tip was "built" strip by strip until the exact streamlined shape, as specified by Hall, was achieved. Notice the ribs to the right of the tip.

. s . This close-up image shows the section of the wing where the aileron would be installed. The two pulleys allowed the cable from the cockpit to move the ailerons up and down. The wing's intricate design, along with diligent work by the Ryan wing department, resulted in an exceptionally strong and structurally advanced wing. Notice how the ribs are tied off with string just prior to covering the wing. This technique holds the ribs straight until the ribs are stitched to the wing's fabric.

(. r . and . s .) Provided by the estate of Donald A. Hall, Sr.

. r .

. s .

. t . A Ryan Airlines employee holds the most important part of the landing gear system, the shock absorber. Built to incorporate eight elastic "bungee" cords, this low tech design allowed the *Spirit* to take off at full weight. The finished and tested shocks could absorb the full force and stress of landing with well over 300 gallons of fuel.

(inset left) Once the shock absorber had been built, it was tested to see how much it could withstand. Stress and maximum load tests were applied, which this special machine could measure (in thousands of pounds). The *Spirit* was estimated to weigh over 5,000 pounds when it took off from New York, so these "simple" shocks had to handle that extreme take-off weight, as well as the force upon landing. Only one plane had ever taken off with such a fuel load, the White Bird that was lost somewhere over the Atlantic along with its two French pilots in 1927.

. u . This seemingly minor part was crafted of special steel tubing heat-treated to withstand extreme forces. Stronger than any other part of the plane, it was integral to the landing gear. The black portion of the lower swing arm (strut) is the axle, which the large wheels would be slipped onto in the final assembly phase.

(. t . and . u .) Provided by the estate of Donald A. Hall, Sr.

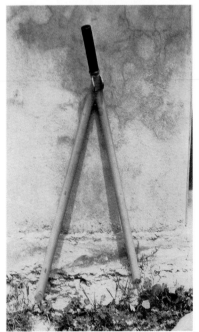

. t .

. u .

. v . As the project neared completion, each newly-produced piece brought the Ryan team a step closer to their goal. This image shows the newly mounted engine section with the oil tank and front fuel tank, which had been removed earlier in the production phase. It finally has been reattached (at left) to the cockpit/tail sections. *Provided by the estate of Donald A. Hall, Sr.*

asembly

"*Each of them*
[men and women]
are striving to do
a quicker and better job
on the Spirit of St. Louis
than they've ever done before.
No pains are too great,
and no hours too long;
lights sometimes burn
in the factory
all through the night."

— CHARLES A. LINDBERGH
The Spirit of St. Louis (1953)

assembly

THE GOVERNMENT HAD RECENTLY REQUIRED AN AVIATOR'S LICENSE AND REGISTRATION NUMBER FOR ANY AIRCRAFT TO BE AUTHORIZED FOR FLIGHT. After the *Spirit of St. Louis* had received its number from the Department of Commerce, "N-X-211" was painted on the wing and tail. "N" marked the *Spirit* as an international aircraft from the United States, while "X" represented the airplane's experimental status. The experimental designation allowed Hall and Lindbergh to make additions or changes to the airplane without explicit permission from the government.

The *Spirit's* initial test flight was scheduled for April 28, 1927. April 27 had been set aside to move the components from the manufacturing facility to the hangar at Dutch Flats 2.5 miles away, where final assembly would take place. Moving the huge custom-designed aircraft proved more challenging than anyone had anticipated. Staying on schedule took every bit of ingenuity and resourcefulness the Ryan team could muster.

From the beginning, the odds had been stacked against the young airmail pilot and the small aircraft company. As the deadline approached, those odds continued to worsen as better-known pilots prepared for their transatlantic attempts in well-tested aircraft. Yet, the possibility of success remained, and the team's enthusiasm was high. They were eager to see the aircraft they had built take flight.

First, they had to find a way to move the aircraft outside the factory. In their haste to build the *Spirit* within the required time frame, Hall, Lindbergh, and the Ryan team had overlooked a few basic problems posed by its increased size and weight. Both the fuselage and wing proved too large to fit through the building's doors.

Undaunted, the Ryan team first focused its attention on the fuselage. The Wright Whirlwind J-5C engine had already been mounted and connected without the propeller. The landing gear and shock absorbers had been mounted, as well. Removing one side of the landing gear allowed the fuselage to be carried by a crew of men to a location just outside the building. The landing gear was reattached to the fuselage while the engine was held aloft by a derrick's crane. The full weight of the *Spirit's* fuselage was carefully released and allowed to rest on the landing gear. After a final inspection, the fuselage was connected tail-first to a company car and towed down Juniper Street to Dutch Flats.

The most difficult component to be transported to Dutch Flats was the wing. The wing's length had been extended by ten feet to accommodate the *Spirit's* increased fuel efficiency and load requirements, so it was too large to be carried out the second-story door onto the stairs. After considering all options, including widening the wing department door, a last thought occurred to the Ryan team. Perhaps they could, instead, take it out the second-story window. Measuring the window and confirming the wing's measurements, they determined it would just fit. But how would they lower the wing to the ground without damaging it?

A railway track ran just outside the factory building, so a boxcar was positioned under the window where the wing would emerge. Carefully, with Lindbergh supervising every step of the operation, several Ryan employees maneuvered the wing out the window and onto the waiting boxcar. Additional men steadied the wing by hand as it sat atop the boxcar. The derrick crane was used to pull the box-car into a position along the street several hundred feet from the building. The crane was then moved to a point behind and to the left of the boxcar and attached to the mid-section of the wing for optimum balance. The wing was cautiously swung out, over, and away from the boxcar. While the wing hovered in mid-air, a team of men pushed the boxcar out of the way as a flatbed truck was moved into position.

With the help of the entire team, the wing was gently lowered onto a padded section of the flatbed. After verifying that the wing's center of gravity was balanced over the truck's rear wheels, it was released from the derrick's crane. Its vertical alignment gave way to a slight angle as the team carefully leaned the wing against the truck's single guardrail for the slow trip to Dutch Flats.

In the hangar at Dutch Flats, the *Spirit*, at last, took form. With its sleek lines and gleaming silver nose, the *Spirit of St. Louis* was like no other plane in existence. Designed and built for a singular flight, it was more than an aircraft. It was a work of art. The next day's test flight would reveal if the aircraft's performance would match its beauty. ⬎

. a .

. a . This image shows the *Spirit's* nose section as it appeared after the rollout from the manufacturing facility's double doors. The landing gear had been too wide to clear the building's doorway, so the right landing gear was removed and reattached once the front section was safely outside. A derrick's crane is holding the *Spirit's* weight from above the engine as the Ryan team attaches the landing gear and verifies its alignment.

. b. In the Spirit's first preview outside the factory, the forward 88-gallon fuel tank and 25-gallon oil tank are visible. The Wright Whirlwind J-5C engine and tanks will remain uncovered until final assembly later that day, when the fishscale-like aluminum cowling at Dutch Flats will enclose the frontal section.

. c. This view from beneath the Wright Whirlwind J-5C engine clearly shows the many cables and lines leading to the engine, the perfect incorporation of the tanks into the frame, and the landing gear's attachment to the fuselage. The fuel and oil lines were specially prepared in sections 18 inches or shorter to resist vibration stresses that could have caused a potentially fatal fuel system problem.

(. a . -. c .) Provided by the estate of Donald A. Hall, Sr.

. c .

. d . In this well-known photograph, taken by Donald Hall, the fuselage is being towed along Juniper Street behind a Ryan company car as it travels from the factory to Dutch Flats. Three Ryan employees man the 1925 Studebaker while Lindbergh rides in Hall's car. The *Spirit's* temporary factory wheels will be replaced with permanent wheels at Dutch Flats later that day. *Provided by the estate of Donald A. Hall, Sr.*

. **e** . The factory workers carefully maneuver the wing out the second-story window onto a boxcar below. Charles Lindbergh, in black and wearing a hat, stands on the roof of the boxcar to the right, overseeing the work. To the lower left of the image is the waiting flatbed truck with its padded guardrail and the separate derrick crane to lift the wing. As the wing is carefully balanced by the Ryan workers, its tight fit through the window is apparent. *Provided by the estate of Donald A. Hall, Sr.*

. f .

. g .

. f . Once it had been moved out of the factory and placed onto the boxcar, the wing was held securely by numerous factory employees. The rented derrick on the left was secured to the boxcar via a cable. The derrick then pulled the boxcar and its precarious load along the railroad tracks. In the photo, you can see the derrick operator looking back as he inches along.

. g . After being pulled past the factory, the boxcar was disengaged from the derrick, leaving the boxcar blocking a side street, which is not clearly visible. The derrick and the crane could then be moved into a better position to carefully lower the wing. A group of men wait as the crane is repositioned. The feet of the men who are holding the wing from the backside can be seen.

. h . In front of the Ryan Airlines factory, the derrick is repositioned behind and to the left of the boxcar as the crane is attached to the midsection of the wing. The derrick's two stabilizers are being set while a team of men continues to hold the wing.

(. f . - . h .) Provided by the estate of Donald A. Hall, Sr.

. h .

. i .

. j .

. k .

. i . & . j . The derrick crane holds the wing while the factory crew pushes and pulls the boxcar clear. Notice the triangular support structure connected to the underside of the wing, which is where the crane is attached. This allowed the wing to remain undamaged while hanging in mid-air.

. k . Once the boxcar had been moved out of harm's way, the crew moved the flatbed truck into position. The truck's wheels are visible beneath the wing and to the right. The crane is still attached to the wing, although it rests securely on the back part of the truck. Once the wing was centered over the flatbed's rear wheels for balance and position, the crane was detached.

(. i . - . k .) Provided by the estate of Donald A. Hall, Sr.

.1. This final image of the flatbed truck and the wing shows a single man on the flatbed as he and the wing begin their 2.5-mile trip to Dutch Flats. The wing has been angled and attached to the truck's guardrail for stability. *Provided by the estate of Donald A. Hall, Sr.*

. m . At Dutch Flats, the Ryan Airlines crew finally had the pleasure of attaching the extra-long wing to the *Spirit's* fuselage. Final assembly took place with a day to spare. *Provided by the estate of Donald A. Hall, Sr.*

Destiny

"The take-off tests
were made at the
abandoned World War I
Camp Kearney,
eleven miles north of
the city of San Diego . . .
located on a mesa,
toward the west, was a
natural surface of
hard-packed clay and rock. "

— Donald A. Hall
The estate of Donald A. Hall, Sr.

Testing

APRIL 28, 1927, WAS A VERY SPECIAL DAY FOR DONALD HALL, CHARLES LINDBERGH, AND THE MEN AND WOMEN OF RYAN AIRLINES. Together, they had invested hundreds of man-hours in the *Spirit of St. Louis* over the previous two months. On that day, the gleaming silver aircraft had been christened and was about to take its first flight. The pilot for whom the aircraft had been designed was in the cockpit at last. As the Ryan team watched and waited, there was an almost palpable sense of anticipation in the air.

The chief mechanic spun the propeller, then moved away as he heard the powerful engine start smoothly. When Lindbergh eased the throttle open, the wheels pushed hard against the chocks. At a nod from Lindbergh, the chocks were pulled, and the *Spirit of St. Louis* taxied onto the field and rolled lightly over the smooth baked-clay surface, gaining speed. Then, with a rush of air, the plane took flight.

The short take-off distance surprised the watching crowd. Chief engineer Donald Hall was ecstatic. The plane he had designed had lifted off the runway in just 6-1/8 seconds and at a distance of 165 feet. Lindbergh pushed the *Spirit* to see how it would handle. Leveling off and opening the throttle, the speed peaked at 128 mph, 3.5 mph faster than expected.

As Lindbergh headed back to Dutch Flats in his custom-designed aircraft, a Navy Hawk fighter approached to take a closer look. The two pilots played in the sky over San Diego for a few moments, spiraling and diving in mock combat. The Hawk was faster, but the *Spirit* maneuvered more easily.

The first of the *Spirit's* many test flights lasted just twenty minutes. After a few adjustments had been made, Lindbergh took her up later in the day to verify that the modifications had corrected the problems. Three more test flights were conducted the following day. On May 3rd, Hall joined Lindbergh as he flew over the beach city. Perched on an armrest inside the cramped cockpit, he snapped the first photographs ever from inside the *Spirit* while in the air. Then Major Erickson, a professional photographer hired by Ryan Airlines, flew with Lindbergh to capture additional images. Erickson followed the *Spirit* in a chase plane later that day to photograph the *Spirit* in flight.

The final speed and fuel load tests were scheduled for May 4, 1927. Following the Army's three-kilometer speed course over San Diego Bay, along Coronado Strand, the *Spirit* again exceeded Hall's calculations by 3.5 mph. At Hall's suggestion, the load tests were completed at Camp Kearney, a site that was perfectly flat, isolated, and unknown to the press. The Ryan team, including Donald Hall and B.F. Mahoney, had assembled by the time the *Spirit* arrived. Hall, Mahoney, and several other Ryan employees walked the field with Lindbergh to pick up the largest of the numerous rocks that littered the site.

The *Spirit* was initially loaded with 70 gallons of fuel. Continuing to add fuel in 50-gallon increments, at first there was no difference in the measured take-off distance. However, once the *Spirit* was moderately loaded, it began to bounce along the surface while small rocks beat against the wheels and landing gear. At 300 gallons, the *Spirit* took to the air in 20 seconds, but the Ryan team wondered how much more strain the tires would be able to handle. The wheel bearings had even begun to smoke a bit. Fearing that 350 gallons would compromise the landing gear, as well as the tires, the remaining planned tests were cancelled. Although Hall would have preferred another point or two on the load data sheet, he could use the existing figures to project the plane's performance curve.

Returning to Dutch Flats, a photo was taken with the entire Ryan team lined up in front of the silver aircraft they had worked so hard to build. A second group photograph was taken with Hawley Bowlus, B.F. Mahoney, Charles Lindbergh, and Donald Hall, the four men who had spearheaded the project. With the tests completed, the *Spirit* had proven itself ready to make the journey for which it had been created. The Ryan team's contribution to Lindbergh's transatlantic attempt was behind them. But their hopes and hearts would travel with the young pilot as he flew the *Spirit of St. Louis* toward its date with destiny. ⌣

. a . Contact! On April 28, 1927, the contact switch was flipped, the propeller was spun, and the magical moment when the *Spirit* would take to the air was about to occur, at last. (Notice the Ryan chief mechanic walking away from the turning propeller as the mighty engine started. "Wrong-Way" Corrigan is standing next to the closed cockpit, ready to pull the chocks.) *Provided by the estate of Donald A. Hall, Sr.*

. **b** . After taxiing down the field, the plane that would eventually break several world records finally takes to the air. The *Spirit of St. Louis* is shown above Dutch Flats, about 2-1/2 miles from the Ryan Airlines facility where it was built. *Provided by the estate of Donald A. Hall, Sr.*

. c .

. d .

. e .

. c . Lindbergh had to get a "feel" for the aircraft and determine its responsiveness. He knew the plane would need adjustment and further testing, but already he was well pleased with its performance and power. Lindbergh remarked that the *Spirit* handled like no other plane he had ever flown.

. d . Banking over the Dutch Flats field after takeoff, the *Spirit* came around over the heads of the Ryan team that had assembled to watch the *Spirit's* first flight. Lindbergh wanted all of them to see how well the aircraft flew and handled.

. e . The *Spirit* comes in for a landing with nose down, as the seemingly blind pilot makes his first attempt at landing the custom-designed aircraft. Lindbergh had no difficulty landing the *Spirit,* and he assured Hall that flying blind wasn't a problem with the amount of flying experience he had.

(. c . - . e .) Provided by the estate of Donald A. Hall, Sr.

.g.

.h.

. f . (opposite page) The first test flight had been completed and the *Spirit of St. Louis* had proven itself. Yes, adjustments had to be made, but the *Spirit* had performed beautifully. Notice the tailskid marks on the field. (The airplane in flight above the *Spirit* is possibly a Curtiss Hawk biplane.)

. g. Hall joined Lindbergh in the small cockpit for a flight over San Diego on May 3, 1927. This image of the instrument panel was snapped by Hall as he sat on the right armrest of the pilot's seat. These were the first photos taken inside the *Spirit* while in flight. When this picture was taken, Lindbergh was banking the plane to the left and flying at full speed.

. h . (top right) This image shows the view from the right window of the *Spirit*. The shock and landing gear are clearly visible, as are the homes of San Diego on the ground. During that flight, Hall took the control stick to get a hands-on feel for the *Spirit's* stability problem.

. i . In this final photo of the aerial view of San Diego, the struts for the wing are clearly visible.

(. f . - . i .) Provided by the estate of Donald A. Hall, Sr.

.i.

Date May 27 Flight _____ Page ____

Time of Take Off _____ Time of landing _____ Duration ____

Weight	Take off Dist.	R.P.M	Air Sp.	Fuel Consump	Oil Temp	Oil Pres.	Alt.	Barom. Pres.	Temp.	Weather	Time	Condition of Field	Wind			
70		1325	80	1:58	35	58	58									
"		1950	125													
110		1925	125													
		1325	80													
150		1375	80													
		1925	123													
200		1950	127		35	58	300			Clear						
		1600	110													
		1500	95													
		1400	80													
		1325	72													
250		1950	126													
		1350	80													

.j. Donald Hall used this log sheet to record the results of the *Spirit's* fuel/load testing. The public was gradually learning more bout the young American pilot who would attempt to fly across the Atlantic, but there were more tests to be completed. With the Ryan team still working in relative secrecy, Hall recommended that the fuel-load tests be performed at Camp Kearney, located on a mesa about 10 miles north of San Diego. (Notice the weight column is actually used to record the amount of fuel.) *Provided by the estate of Donald A. Hall, Sr.*

. k .

. l .

. m .

. k . (top left) Camp Kearney included a parade ground for the military. It was not an airfield, but the remote location and long, flat areas made it work well for the sequential fuel-load tests. The surface, however, was quite rocky, in contrast to Dutch Flats' smooth mud surface. Notice the fuel barrels stacked next to the *Spirit*.

. l . As fuel was added in 50-gallon increments, the *Spirit* initially had no problem with takeoff. Once the *Spirit* was moderately loaded, however, the roughness of the field began to worry Lindbergh, Hall, and Mahoney. To avoid damaging the landing gear and tires, the remaining load tests beyond 300 gallons were cancelled.

. m . As the fuel load was increased, it became more and more difficult to get the *Spirit* airborne from the rock-strewn field. Still within the performance range for which Hall had designed the aircraft, the tests were stopped at 300 gallons of fuel. A blown tire could have ended the entire project. Rather than risking an accident under greater fuel loads, Hall felt he could project the remaining take-off performance curves for 350 and 400 gallons from the existing test data and results.

(. k . - . m .) *Provided by the estate of Donald A. Hall, Sr.*

. n .

. o .

. p .

. n . This photo, taken from inside a chase plane, shows the *Spirit* in flight over San Diego. The city of San Diego can be seen faintly in the background.

. o . In an image from the "Spirit First Flight" footage, the *Spirit* is seen soaring over the ocean with the city of San Diego in the background.

. p . This image of the *Spirit* in flight over San Diego was taken by Major Erickson, a well-known aerial photographer. The thin tubes sticking up from the wing are vents for the fuel tanks and caps removed when re-fueling the tanks.

(. n . - . p .) Provided by the estate of Donald A. Hall, Sr.

. q . On May 10, 1927, Lindbergh was ready to start the first leg of his trip to New York. After taking off for his historic flight to St. Louis, he was followed for a time by four members of the Ryan team in a Ryan chase plane. Those four included Donald Hall, Hawley Bowlus, A.J. Edwards, and pilot Harrigan. Hall took this photo of the *Spirit* from inside the chase plane.

. r . The *Spirit* is shown banking around to head east as Lindbergh takes the next step toward the transatlantic flight and fulfillment of the dream the Ryan team in San Diego had worked so hard to help him achieve.

. s . The plane that would attempt the "impossible" is shown flying over the mountains of Southern California as it heads off alone toward the Borrego Desert. Shortly after this image was taken, the four members of the Ryan team who had helped create the Spirit turned back toward San Diego, but their hopes and prayers traveled east with Charles Lindbergh.

(. q . - . s .) Provided by the estate of Donald A. Hall, Sr.

. q .

. r .

. s .

NEW YORK TO PARIS
PLANE IN FLIGHT

. t . In these images from the first flight footage, the three men who spearheaded the project, Donald Hall, B.F. Mahoney, and Charles Lindbergh, pose in front of the *Spirit*. In one image, Hall and Lindbergh shake hands for the camera.

. u . **(opposite page)** The four principals involved in the *Spirit* project pose in front of the aircraft they helped build. From left to right are Hawley Bowlus (factory manager), B.F. Mahoney (president of Ryan Airlines), Charles Lindbergh (pilot), and Donald Hall, Sr. (chief engineer/designer).

(. t . & . u .) Provided by the estate of Donald A. Hall, Sr.

. v . Assembled in front of the *Spirit of St. Louis* is the entire crew that built the airplane and made it a success. Toward the left (near the end of the propeller) is Lindbergh, with his famous crushed hat. Known for his wonderful sense of humor, he was appreciated by everyone at Ryan. Hall is fourth from the right. *Provided by the estate of Donald A. Hall, Sr.*

SPIRIT — THE TRIBUTE

Spirit of St. Louis

May 20-21, 1927

*"The long, narrow runway
stretches out ahead.
Over the telephone wires
at its end lies the
Atlantic Ocean;
and beyond that,
mythical as the
rainbow's pot of gold,
Europe and Paris."*

— CHARLES A. LINDBERGH
The Spirit of St. Louis (1953)

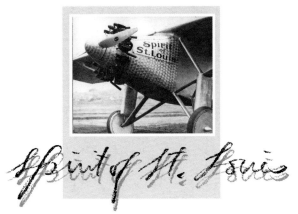

MAY 20-21, 1927

WHEN LINDBERGH TOUCHED DOWN AT LE BOURGET AIRFIELD, 100,000 FRENCH CITIZENS WHO HAD EAGERLY AWAITED HIS ARRIVAL PUSHED DOWN THE BARRICADES AND RUSHED THE STILL-MOVING SPIRIT OF ST. LOUIS. Lindbergh feared that the cheering crowd would crush him and his now-famous airplane. Eventually, he was extricated from the throng and taken to meet with U.S. Ambassador Herrick. Happy, but exhausted, the pilot most wanted a meal, a bed, and assurance that the *Spirit* was safe. He soon had all three. When sleep finally overtook him, Lindbergh had been awake for 63 hours straight.

From the moment he landed in France, Lindbergh became a hero in the eyes of the world. His life was about to change in ways he could not have anticipated. From Paris, the record-breaking pilot flew the *Spirit of St. Louis* to Belgium and then on to England, where he was honored as the monarchy's official guest. In England, the Royal Air Force carefully dismantled the *Spirit* for its trip back to the United States aboard the USS cruiser Memphis on June 4.

When the Memphis docked in Washington, D.C., on June 11, Donald Hall was waiting to congratulate his friend and photograph the cruiser and its cargo as it was unloaded. The huge crate containing the *Spirit* was taken to Bolling Field near Washington and reassembled so that Lindbergh could fly the plane to New York for the official award dinner. While in Washington, the record-breaking pilot was given the first Distinguished Flying Cross ever awarded.

Lindbergh's first attempt to fly the *Spirit* after it had been reassembled at Bolling field was disappointing. The engine didn't sound right to the experienced flyer, so he instead entertained the waiting crowd with acrobatics in a borrowed Curtiss P-1 biplane. After engine repairs had been completed a few days later, Lindbergh returned to Bolling Field to fly the *Spirit* to Roosevelt Field for a June 16 ceremony attended by 25,000 well-wishers. That evening, the coveted Orteig Prize was presented to Charles Lindbergh at a gala dinner in New York.

Donald Hall attended the dinner, along with the most prestigious of New York City's elite. During Lindbergh's address, he asked Hall to stand so that the assembled guests could meet the man who had made the *Spirit's* flight possible. While Hall felt honored by this public recognition, even more special to him was an invitation from the Mayor of Brooklyn for Hall and Lindbergh to attend a special ceremony in Hall's home town.

The morning after the Orteig dinner, Lindbergh flew the *Spirit* to the city of St. Louis to attend a series of celebrations arranged by the *Spirit's* investors. Hall remained in Brooklyn to visit family and friends before returning to San Diego.

By July 1, Lindbergh had begun an air tour across the United States in the *Spirit of St. Louis*, making a total of 82 stops. The Daniel Guggenheim Fund for the Promotion of Aeronautics funded the tour to demonstrate the safety and viability of air travel. Later, that tour was extended to include Mexico, where Lindbergh met his future wife, and other Central American countries before ending in Washington, D.C. The beautiful aircraft and its attractive young pilot easily captivated the public's imagination. However, the lines between fact and fiction blurred as the story of the flight became a modern legend.

Although postal regulations dictated that no living American could be memorialized on a postage stamp, the rule was set aside in the case of Lindbergh's accomplishment. The *Spirit's* airmail stamp was issued exactly four weeks after its flight across the Atlantic, making Lindbergh the first living person to have his name mentioned on an American stamp.

In 1928, the beautiful aircraft that Lindbergh, Hall, and the Ryan team had worked so hard to build was donated to the Smithsonian Institution. It was put on permanent display in Washington, D.C., joining another famous aircraft, the Kitty Hawk bi-plane built by Orville and Wilbur Wright.

.a. Lindbergh pictured with the *Spirit,* post NYP. *Courtesy of Dan Clemons.*

.b. Portrait of Lindbergh in the cockpit of a Ryan M-1. *Provided by the estate of Donald A. Hall, Sr.*

.c. Charles Lindbergh at Curtiss Field in NYC. *Courtesy of Dan Clemons.*

.a.

.b.

.c.

5.30 A.M. EDITION

TODAY'S WEATHER FORECAST
Cooler, cloudy, bright spells, rain.
Wind NW to N, moderate.
Temperature yesterday: Max. 17
(63 Fahr.), min. 9 (48 Fahr.).
Channel crossings: Rather rough.

TODAY'S ISSUE: 16 PAGES, 2 SECTIONS

5.30 A.M. EDITION

THE NEW YORK HERALD
EUROPEAN EDITION OF THE NEW YORK HERALD TRIBUNE

EXCHANGE RATES (CABLES)
Dollar in Paris - - - 25fr. 54 1/2c.
Dollar in London - - - - - 4s. 2d.
Dollar in Berlin (gold mk) 4m. 21p5
Dollar in Rome - - - - 18 lire 30c.
Pound in Paris - - - - 124fr. 02c.

40th YEAR. No. 14,477.   Business Office and Information Bureau: 49 AVENUE DE L'OPERA. Tel.: Gutenberg 04-28 and 28-15.   PARIS, SUNDAY, MAY 22, 1927.   Editorial Office: 38 RUE DU LOUVRE. Tel.: Gutenberg 03-18 and 03-12.   PRICE: Paris and France, .70c.

LINDBERGH ARRIVES ON RECORD-BREAKING FLIGHT

. d . (opposite page) A crowd of well-wishers gather around the *Spirit* at Curtiss Field before Lindbergh's takeoff. *Courtesy of the San Diego Aerospace Museum.*

. e . Headlines from *The New York Herald,* European Edition — Paris, Sunday, May 22, 1927. *Provided by the estate of Donald A. Hall, Sr.*

. f . [image detail] Crowd at Le Bourget airfield waiting for Charles A. Lindbergh's arrival shortly at 10 p.m. on May 21, 1927. *Courtesy of the Missouri Historical Society, St. Louis. Henri Manuel, photographer.*

. g . As Lindbergh landed the *Spirit* at Le Bourget, the waiting crowd rushed onto the airfield. *Courtesy of Corbis Images.*

. h . Charles Lindbergh and U.S. Ambassador Myron T. Herrick. *Courtesy of Corbis Images.*

. i . Charles Lindbergh waving the American and French flags from the American Embassy in Paris. *Courtesy of Corbis Images.*

.j. **(top left)** The cruiser USS Memphis symbolized the greatness of the American Naval power in 1927. The crate containing the *Spirit of St. Louis* is clearly visible on the forward deck, directly in front of the bridge. *Provided by the estate of Donald A. Hall, Sr.*

(top right) The USS Memphis was the Admiral's flagship for the Atlantic fleet, sent to England by President Coolidge to return America's newest hero and his *Spirit* to the United States for a grand homecoming celebration. The *Spirit of St. Louis* had been dismantled and crated for the trip back to Washington D.C. *Provided by the estate of Donald A. Hall, Sr.*

(bottom left) Lindbergh deboarding the USS Memphis as it docks at the Washington Naval Yard. *Courtesy of Lindbergh Picture Collection, Yale Library.*

. k . Once the USS Memphis arrived in Washington, D.C., its special cargo was transferred to a steamboat/barge and taken to the dock. Using a series of guidelines and pulleys, the crew prepared to move the crate containing the *Spirit of St. Louis* back onto American soil.

. l . After the *Spirit* had been unloaded, it was reassembled at Bolling Field and prepared for flight. Lindbergh later wrote that he had not wanted the *Spirit* to be put into a crate for shipment home. He had, however, few choices beyond flying it back.

(. k . & . l .) Provided by the estate of Donald A. Hall, Sr.

. l .

. m .

. n .

. l . Lindbergh was given a hero's welcome everywhere. *Courtesy of Corbis Images.*

. m . President Coolidge awards the distinguished Flying Cross to Lindbergh at the Washington Monument. *Courtesy of Corbis Images.*

. n . In addition to the huge tickertape parade up Broadway, Lindbergh was an honored guest at festivities hosted in Brooklyn, Hall's hometown. Here, Hall (far left, top) and Lindbergh are pictured on June 17th. *Provided by the estate of Donald A. Hall, Sr.*

. p . On June 16, Charles Lindbergh and Donald Hall attended this gala dinner in New York where Lindbergh received the coveted Orteig prize. Lindbergh and Hall are standing at the head table below the largest Stars & Stripes banner in the background. *Provided by the estate of Donald A. Hall, Sr.*

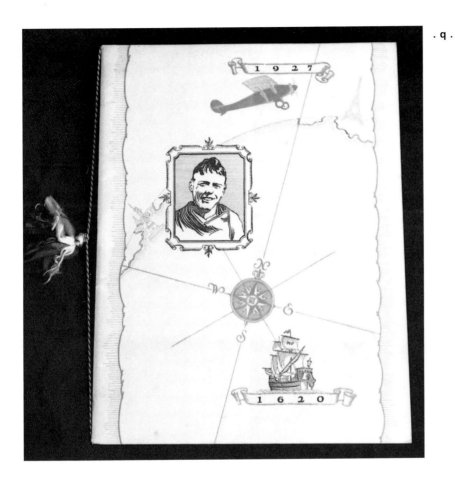

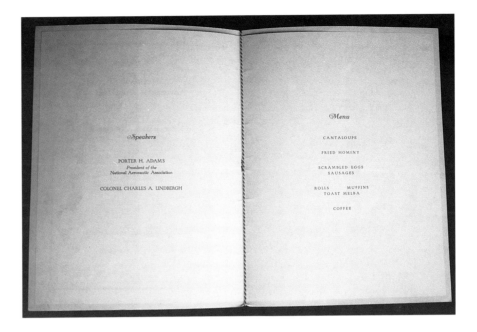

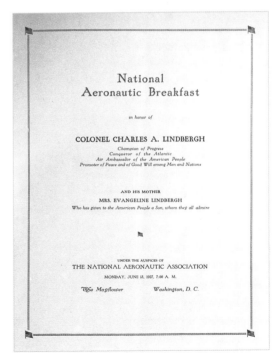

. q . Pictured is the menu from the June 13, 1927, National Aeronautical Association honorary breakfast held for Charles Lindbergh at the Mayflower Hotel in Washington, D.C. Donald Hall also attended the celebration.

. r . Charles Lindbergh and his mother, Mrs. Evangeline Lindbergh, were honored guests at the special breakfast.

. s . This unused match book was one of many collectables presented on June 14 to commemorate Charles Lindbergh's accomplishment.

(. q . - . s .) Provided by the estate of Donald A. Hall, Sr.

. t . Four weeks after the *Spirit's* flight across the Atlantic, a special airmail stamp was rushed through the US Postal Service. It proved to be one of the most popular stamps ever printed. The *Spirit's* 1927 airmail stamp marked a special departure for the USPS, as postal regulations clearly stated that no living American could be memorialized on a postage stamp. An exception was granted, and Lindbergh became the first person to have his name honored on an American stamp during his lifetime. **(inset)** In 1931, Donald Hall copyrighted his company logo, which was patterned after the famous stamp. *Provided by the estate of Donald A. Hall, Sr.*

SPIRIT — THE AFTERMATH

184

[signature] N. A. Hall

The Aftermath

"...My grandfather believed that through hard work, dedication, and an understanding of the forces around us, anything is possible. "

— NOVA HALL
Grandson, Donald A. Hall, Sr.

The Aftermath

THE SUCCESSFUL TRANSATLANTIC FLIGHT OF THE SPIRIT OF ST. LOUIS OPENED A NEW CHAPTER IN AVIATION AND MADE CHARLES LINDBERGH ONE OF THE MOST FAMOUS MEN IN HISTORY. For Donald Hall, everything had changed and, yet, very little was different. His creativity and engineering skills had been put to the test, and he had far surpassed all expectations. He knew that he had played a key part in history and was pleased with his contribution. But, as the fervor and the media followed the charismatic young pilot on his cross-country tour, Donald Hall was slowly left behind. He and the Ryan team moved on to other projects in the same factory in San Diego.

Hall missed the intense collaboration he had enjoyed with Charles Lindbergh while the *Spirit* was being designed and built. The two men had developed a strong bond. Before the flight, they had often talked of starting their own experimental aircraft company, with Hall as the designer and Lindbergh as the test pilot. When Lindbergh was swept away by his unexpected fame, that dream faded. Then, in 1929, Ryan Airlines became Mahoney-Ryan Airlines and relocated to St. Louis. Although Mahoney asked Hall to move with the company, the talented engineer had no desire to leave San Diego. So he remained in the city he had come to love.

Hall made plans to start his own company without Lindbergh. In 1932, he incorporated Hall Aeronautical Research & Development Company with a financial backer from the East Coast. He began work on his Hall X-1 prototype. This aircraft far exceeded the *Spirit's* accomplishments in terms of safety, capabilities, and performance. It was exceptionally stable and could fly straight and level with no one at the controls. Many years before the development of automatic pilot, this was a major accomplishment. The Hall X-1 was also fast and highly maneuverable. It could self-adjust to a load placed anywhere in the fuselage. An experimental aircraft, the Hall X-1 was built to test the new tandem wing design Hall had pioneered and patented.

Just as Hall was about to realize success, the company experienced partnership and funding problems. Although Hall retained the manufacturing facility and ownership of his designs, there was insufficient cash to maintain the operation. So, he closed Hall Aeronautical and took a job with Consolidated Aircraft Corporation, which had relocated to San Diego. Donald Hall had a family to support, and that took precedence over his dream of pioneering a new class of aircraft.

In 1933, Hall had married the beautiful Elizabeth Walker, a schoolteacher he had met three years earlier. Elizabeth gave birth to their only child, Donald Albert Hall, Jr., a year later. Throughout their lives they lived in Point Loma, north of San Diego, in a home that Hall had designed. Donald Hall was a good husband and a good father. His devotion to family was the cornerstone of his life.

Hall's professional life was disappointing for several years after he closed his company. During the Depression the aviation industry, along with the rest of the country, receded. Without the personal wealth necessary to develop his many advanced designs, including flying wings and gull-winged aircraft, Hall was forced to work for other aircraft companies. As a cutting-edge engineer and designer with a unique vision, accepting any position except that of chief engineer seemed like a step back.

While working for Convair during the war years, Hall became an executive in the company when he was promoted to patent director. He played a significant role in the design of the B-24 Liberator and other aircraft advancements. When the European war ended, Hall was asked to join a contingent of aircraft experts traveling to Europe as part of a classified mission to learn about the German Luftwaffe advances. After the war had ended, the military industrial complex was rocked by huge cutbacks. Donald Hall was laid off when Convair eliminated thousands of jobs.

While still looking for a position in his field, Hall went to Los Angeles where he worked briefly as an engineer for an oil company. Eventually, he returned to the work he loved, pioneering new forms of aviation. In 1952, Hall was appointed head of the Navy's new helicopter branch at North Island, San Diego. He worked there until his retirement in 1963, providing valuable research and engineering analysis for gyro-aircraft.

With time, Donald Hall's connection to the *Spirit of St. Louis* faded into the background. But his role in the historical event was not totally overlooked. In 1957, Hall was asked to serve as technical advisor for the Hollywood movie, "The Spirit of St. Louis," starring James Stewart as the young airmail pilot. Then, a year before his death, Donald Hall took part in a special ceremony at North Island to honor the 40th Anniversary of the *Spirit*.

Hall died in 1968 following a heart attack. As he had requested, news of his death was not released to the media until a week had passed so the family would have time to mourn privately. As always, Hall's family had been his primary consideration. Elizabeth contacted Charles Lindbergh personally to tell him of his old friend's death.

Although unable to maintain the closeness they had enjoyed at Ryan, Hall and Lindbergh continued their friendship through correspondence, phone calls, and occasional visits. Over the years, Hall was the recipient of several gifts from Charles Lindbergh and Anne Morrow Lindbergh, including a specially designed lighter engraved, "To Donald Hall from CA Lindbergh." Hall treasured this silver lighter, which matched the color of the *Spirit*.

Although his technical ability was undeniable, in the end, Donald Hall was defined more by his strength of character than by his engineering masterpiece. He was best described as a loyal friend and devoted family man who delighted in photography and the wonders of nature. His life, both before and after the *Spirit's* flight, was based on the same principles that built the *Spirit of St. Louis*: integrity, creativity, ingenuity, and responsibility. Nevertheless, the airplane that Donald Hall designed in 1927 changed the course of aviation history. The legacy of the man who designed this extraordinary aircraft lives on in every airplane that takes flight.

Designing the "Spirit of St. Louis"

By DONALD A. HALL, M'19, Chief Engineer & Designer, Ryan Airlines

For two months these two modest young men worked side by side in the same room, the one solving aerial navigational problems in advance, the other designing The One Best Machine to meet the requirements of the pilot and of the untried voyage. Did they succeed? . . DID they!!

ON February 26, 1927 Colonel Charles A. Lindbergh (then Captain) arrived in San Diego for the purpose of setting forth to the Ryan Airlines his ideas on securing a plane in which he might successfully compete for the Orteig prize for the first New York to Paris flight. A conference attended by Colonel Lindbergh, Mr. B. Franklin Mahoney, President of the Ryan Airlines, and the writer was at once held, and plans were formulated for designing a monoplane which could make such a flight.

There are a number of unusual problems to be met in designing a plane of the characteristics possessed by the

What "Lindy" thinks of "Don"

(Extract from report of reception by Aeronautical Chamber of Commerce, Waldorf-Astoria Hotel, New York— N. Y. Times, June 17, 1927.)

Refers to Plane's Designer

Colonel Lindbergh then gave another illustration of his modesty and desire to give full credit to others, which have marked him since he became famous, by referring to Donald Hall, designer of his plane.

"There is one person to whom great credit belongs," he continued. "He is Donald Hall. I am going to ask him to rise so that you may see another one of the partnership, 'we.'"

Mr. Hall, a slender young man, arose with a smile blushing. Enthusiastic applause greeted him.

"Spirit of St. Louis." Perhaps the first and most important of these unusual considerations was that of a good power reserve on takeoff, and it was this that caused considerable thought, although after careful consideration this problem was adequately met, as will hereinafter be set forth. The other problems of design which are novel are (1) those of locating the pilot in a point of maximum safety; (2) that of providing sufficient space for a gasoline capacity for a 3,600 mile flight; (3) that of providing a landing gear which would be capable of withstanding the strains and stresses occasioned by both taking off and landing with full load; (4) that of designing a structure capable of supporting the unusually heavy load with a sufficient load factor; and many other minor details which the writer will not endeavor to discuss in this brief article.

Unusually large wings for this size airplane are provided to derive sufficient lift to carry the heavy load and to give sufficient power reserve, since, in general, the lifting power is directly proportional to the wing area of the plane. At the start of the New York to Paris flight the wing loading was 16.5 lbs. per sq. ft., which is, of course, the weight of the airplane per square foot of wing surface.

To meet Colonel Lindbergh's requirement of safety for the pilot, the main or central gasoline tank is located forward of the pilot's cabin. Directly to the rear of the motor is a 25 gallon

oil tank which provides an excellent fire-wall to protect the fuselage gasoline tanks, which are directly aft therefrom, from fire hazard, and the pilot is thus placed in a position of maximum safety from possible injury due to being crushed by gasoline tanks in case of any possible landing accident.

The gasoline tanks are composed of a forward tank of 88 gallon capacity (above described) located behind the oil tank, and to the rear of this tank is the main or central tank of 210 gallon capacity. In the wing structure are three tanks with a total capacity of 152 gallons. All tanks connect with a Lunkenheimer distributor in the pilot's cabin which distributes fuel from any tank to the carburetor, and it is also possible to pump gasoline from any one tank to any other tank. Connecting with the engine are two separate fuel systems for safety in case of stoppage or a leak in any one system.

In each issue we present an exclusive technical article by a Pratt Tech man identified with a recent engineering achievement of major importance. Last time it was "Trans-oceanic Radio Telephony," by Lloyd Espenschied, E'09, the "father" of that development. A few weeks ago we thought of leaving out technical articles from the Anniversary Issue . . . but we rather changed our mind when THIS volplane gracefully out of the azure.

TECHNICAL PREPARATION OF THE RYAN NEW YORK-PARIS AIRPLANE

By Donald A. Hall
Designer of the NY-P Monoplane Chief Engineer, Ryan Airlines, Inc.

THE development of the Ryan NY-P airplane was begun with the idea of using a standard model Ryan M-2 and making modifications to suit the special purpose of a flight from New York to Paris. Upon Colonel Lindbergh's arrival at the factory on February 26, it was quickly determined that modification of the M-2 was less practicable than developing a new design. Colonel Lindbergh laid out the following basic specifications: that the airplane should be a monoplane type; powered with a single Wright J-5-C engine; have a good power reserve on take-off when carrying more than 400 gallons of gasoline; and, must have the pilot located in rear of all tanks for safety in a forced landing.

The decision on these basic specifications immediately determined the inadvisability of using the standard Ryan M-2 model. The design of the airplane was then laid out anew, the fuselage model approximately in regard to design and structure, but being lengthened two feet. The fuselage structure was designed for full load to suitable load factors for full loading in flying and landing conditions. A split axle chassis was designed to a four load factor at full designed load. The wing structure was designed to suitable load factors in high incidence, low incidence and diving conditions at full load.

Colonel Lindbergh took a very active interest in the design of the airplane and he closely cooperated with me throughout the entire construction of the plane. The location of the pilot's cockpit (cabin) in the rear of the fuselage and entirely enclosed, which is the most radical feature of the design, had its development based on the primary requisite of safety, it being considered that in the event of an accident the pilot would be in the safest possible position. The disadvantages as regards visibility were quickly decided to be of relatively minor importance.

The periscope was suggested by Mr. Randolph, of the Ryan Airlines, who had considerable submarine experience. This suggestion was accepted by Colonel Lindbergh with the limitation that if it was not satisfactory or had any aerodynamical disadvantage it would be discarded at New York. The periscope con-

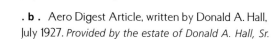

Colonel Chas. A. Lindbergh and Donald A. Hall.

The instrument board of the Ryan NY-P.

sists of a panel in the instrument board through which a view directly forward is afforded by an angular mirror. It has a frontal size of about three by five inches, which projects from the left side of the fuselage, and which can be retracted when not in use. The device proved of no disadvantage aerodynamically on account of the retractable feature, and was of certain utility during flight.

To ensure proper balance the engine was of necessity moved forward considerably. The additional space in the forward part of fuselage, which was provided by this extension, was utilized for the oil tank, located directly in the rear of the engine and a gasoline tank was located in the rear of the oil tank. The oil and tank provided an excellent fire wall. It was found that with full load the two tanks, although so far forward, did not interfere with the trim of the airplane to an extent which could not readily be taken care of by the adjustable stabilizer.

All of the various items of design had the most careful consideration, in which Colonel Lindbergh took a prominent part. The interest shown by him in the detailed design of the airplane was in no way a critical interest. Colonel Lindbergh's time was further occupied during the period in which the airplane was under construction in a careful and intensive study of navigation. This study was most complete. During four weeks practically all his waking hours were occupied by this study of navigation and the preparation of charts and data for use in a dead reckoning flight. It should be borne in mind that he had practically no technical knowledge of the art of navigation prior to this time with the exception of such aerial navigation as he had had in his Army and Air Mail experience.

Members of the Ryan Airlines factory organization who were responsible for the construction of the airplane are Mr. B. Franklin Mahoney, president of the company; Mr. W. H. Bowlus, factory manager; Mr. Bert Tindale, shop superintendent and in charge of wing department; Mr. Walter Locke, in charge of purchasing department, who also assisted in engineering; and the following men in charge of their various departments—Mr. McNeal (final assembly): Mr. Fred Rohr (tank and

---

. **a** . Pratt Institute Article written by Donald A. Hall, July 1927. *Provided by the estate of Donald A. Hall, Sr.*

. **b** . Aero Digest Article, written by Donald A. Hall, July 1927. *Provided by the estate of Donald A. Hall, Sr.*

. c . In 1933, Hall finally obtained the funding he needed to fulfill his dream of starting a new aeronautical research company specializing in design and development. Named Hall Aeronautical Development Co., the company was founded just as the Depression took hold in 1931. The US Copyright Office approved his special logo, "The Spirit of St. Louis, Designed by Donald Hall," the same year. *Provided by the estate of Donald A. Hall, Sr.*

. d . **(top left)** The Hall X-1 taxis in from the field, with Hall sitting in the front and pilot Harrigan in the back seat.

(top right) The Hall X-1 was a technologically advanced plane that exhibited economy, maneuverability, performance, and safety. The design, which Hall had patented, could fly with no one at the controls. Built many years before the first automatic pilot, the Hall X-1 represented the beginnings of a new form of airplane design.

(bottom right) Hall, test pilot Harrigan, and Hall's engineering assistant pose in front of the Hall X-1, a highly advanced aircraft design for the 1930's.

. e . **(opposite page)** Donald Hall pictured with his Tandem wing test bed design, the Hall X-1. *Provided by the estate of Donald A. Hall, Sr.*

Provided by the estate of Donald A. Hall, Sr.

40 POPULAR SCIENCE MONTHLY February, 1929

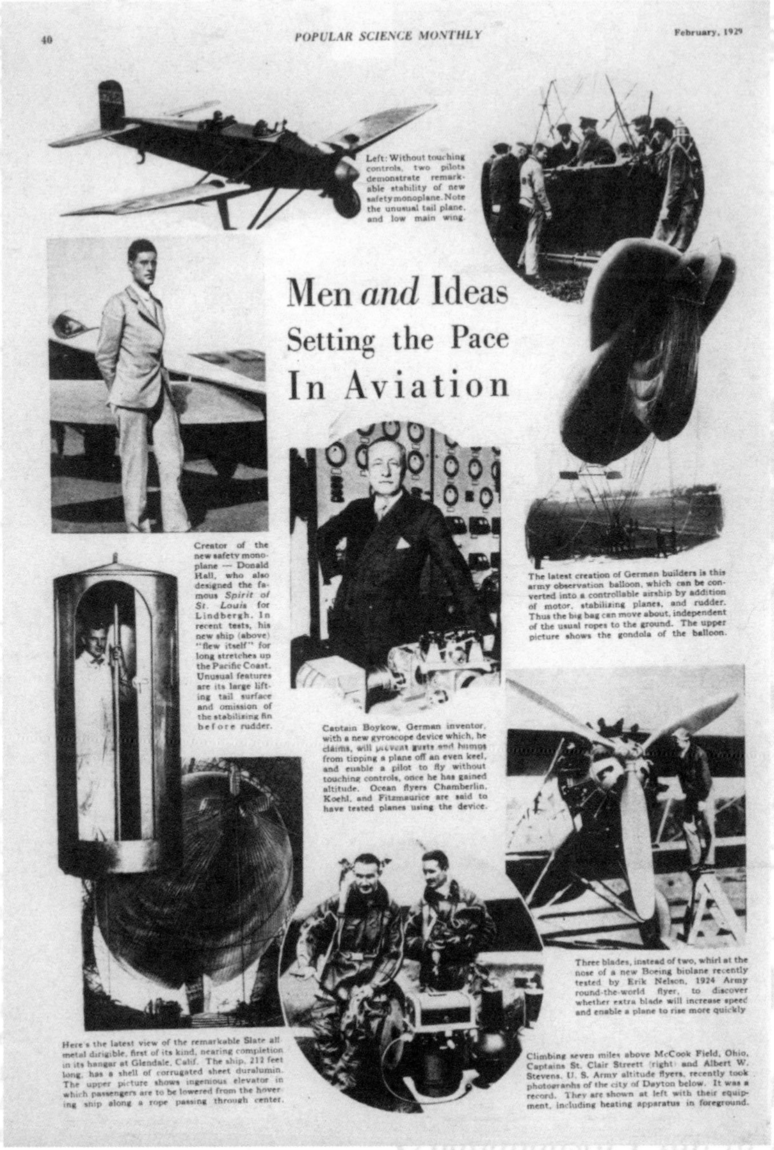

Men *and* Ideas Setting the Pace In Aviation

Left: Without touching controls, two pilots demonstrate remarkable stability of new safety monoplane. Note the unusual tail plane, and low main wing.

Creator of the new safety monoplane — Donald Hall, who also designed the famous *Spirit of St. Louis* for Lindbergh. In recent tests, his new ship (above) "flew itself" for long stretches up the Pacific Coast. Unusual features are its large lifting tail surface and omission of the stabilizing fin before rudder.

The latest creation of German builders is this army observation balloon, which can be converted into a controllable airship by addition of motor, stabilizing planes, and rudder. Thus the big bag can move about, independent of the usual ropes to the ground. The upper picture shows the gondola of the balloon.

Captain Boykow, German inventor, with a new gyroscope device which, he claims, will prevent gusts and bumps from tipping a plane off an even keel, and enable a pilot to fly without touching controls, once he has gained altitude. Ocean flyers Chamberlin, Koehl, and Fitzmaurice are said to have tested planes using the device.

Three blades, instead of two, whirl at the nose of a new Boeing biplane recently tested by Erik Nelson, 1924 Army round-the-world flyer, to discover whether extra blade will increase speed and enable a plane to rise more quickly

Here's the latest view of the remarkable Slate all metal dirigible, first of its kind, nearing completion in its hangar at Glendale, Calif. The ship, 212 feet long, has a shell of corrugated sheet duralumin. The upper picture shows ingenious elevator in which passengers are to be lowered from the hovering ship along a rope passing through center.

Climbing seven miles above McCook Field, Ohio, Captains St. Clair Streett (right) and Albert W. Stevens, U. S. Army altitude flyers, recently took photographs of the city of Dayton below. It was a record. They are shown at left with their equipment, including heating apparatus in foreground.

NEWS OF SOUTHERN

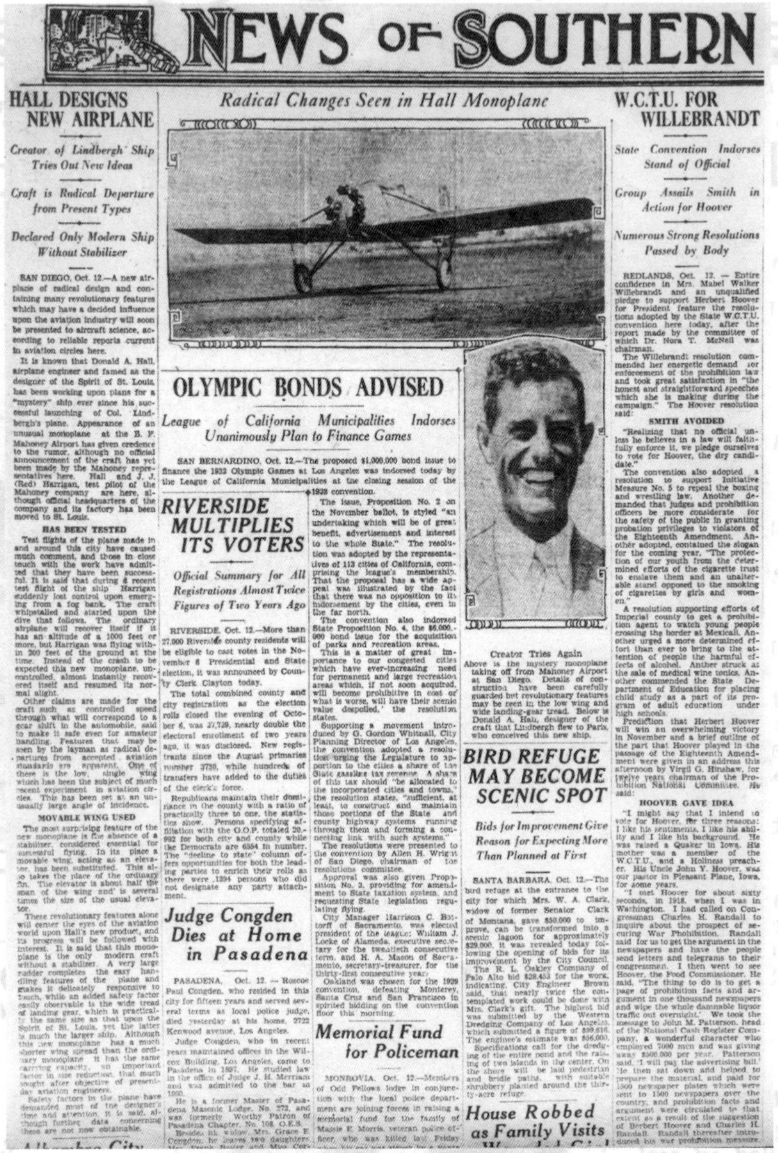

HALL DESIGNS NEW AIRPLANE

Creator of Lindbergh' Ship Tries Out New Ideas

Craft is Radical Departure from Present Types

Declared Only Modern Ship Without Stabilizer

SAN DIEGO, Oct. 12.—A new airplane of radical design and containing many revolutionary features which may have a decided influence upon the aviation industry will soon be presented to aircraft science, according to reliable reports current in aviation circles here.

It is known that Donald A. Hall, airplane engineer and famed as the designer of the Spirit of St. Louis, has been working upon plans for a "mystery" ship ever since his successful launching of Col. Lindbergh's plane. Appearance of an unusual monoplane at the B. F. Mahoney Airport has given credence to the rumor, although no official announcement of the craft has yet been made by the Mahoney representatives here. Hall and J. J. (Red) Harrigan, test pilot of the Mahoney company are here, although official headquarters of the company and its factory has been moved to St. Louis.

HAS BEEN TESTED

Test flights of the plane made in and around this city have caused much comment, and those in close touch with the work have admitted that they have been successful. It is said that during a recent test flight of the ship Harrigan suddenly lost control upon emerging from a fog bank. The craft whipstalled and started upon the dive that follows. The ordinary airplane will recover itself if it has an altitude of a 1000 feet or more, but Harrigan was flying within 200 feet of the ground at the time. Instead of the crash to be expected this new monoplane, uncontrolled, almost instantly recovered itself and resumed its normal alight.

Other claims are made for the craft such as controlled speed through what will correspond to a gear shift in the automobile, said to make it safe even for amateur handling. Features that may be seen by the layman as radical departures from accepted aviation standards are apparent. One of these is the low, single wing which has been the subject of much recent experiment in aviation circles. This has been set at an unusually large angle of incidence.

MOVABLE WING USED

The most surprising feature of the new monoplane is the absence of a stabilizer, considered essential for successful flying. In its place a movable wing, acting as an elevator, has been substituted. This also takes the place of the ordinary fin. The elevator is about half the span of the wing and is several times the size of the usual elevator.

These revolutionary features alone will center the eyes of the aviation world upon Hall's new product, and its progress will be followed with interest. It is said that this monoplane is the only modern craft without a stabilizer. A very large rudder completes the easy handling features of the plane and makes it delicately responsive to touch, while an added safety factor easily observable is the wide tread of landing gear, which is practically the same size as that upon the Spirit of St. Louis, yet the latter is much the larger ship. Although this new monoplane has a much shorter wing spread than the ordinary monoplane it has the same carrying capacity, an important factor in size reduction, that much sought after objective of present-day aviation engineers.

Safety factors in the plane have demanded most of the designer's time and attention, it is said, although further data concerning these are not now obtainable.

Radical Changes Seen in Hall Monoplane

OLYMPIC BONDS ADVISED

League of California Municipalities Indorses Unanimously Plan to Finance Games

SAN BERNARDINO, Oct. 12.—The proposed $1,000,000 bond issue to finance the 1932 Olympic Games at Los Angeles was indorsed today by the League of California Municipalities at the closing session of the 1928 convention.

The issue, Proposition No. 2 on the November ballot, is styled "an undertaking which will be of great benefit, advertisement and interest to the whole State." The resolution was adopted by the representatives of 113 cities of California, comprising the league's membership. That the proposal has a wide appeal was illustrated by the fact that there was no opposition to its indorsement by the cities, even in the far north.

The convention also indorsed State Proposition No. 4, the $6,000,000 bond issue for the acquisition of parks and recreation areas.

This is a matter of great importance to our congested cities which have ever-increasing need for permanent and large recreation areas which, if not soon acquired, will become prohibitive in cost or what is worse, will have their scenic value despoiled," the resolution states.

Supporting a movement introduced by G. Gordon Whitnall, City Planning Director of Los Angeles, the convention adopted a resolution urging the Legislature to apportion to the cities a share of the State gasoline tax revenue. A share of this tax should "be allocated to the incorporated cities and towns," the resolution states, "sufficient, at least, to construct and maintain those portions of the State and county highway systems running through them and forming a connecting link with such systems."

The resolutions were presented to the convention by Allen H. Wright of San Diego, chairman of the resolutions committee.

Approval was also given Proposition No. 3, providing for amendment to State taxation system, and requesting State legislation regulating flying.

City Manager Harrison C. Bottorff of Sacramento, was elected president of the league; William J. Locke of Alameda, executive secretary for the twentieth consecutive term, and H. A. Mason of Sacramento, secretary-treasurer, for the thirty-first consecutive year.

Oakland was chosen for the 1929 convention, defeating Monterey, Santa Cruz and San Francisco in spirited bidding on the convention floor this morning.

RIVERSIDE MULTIPLIES ITS VOTERS

Official Summary for All Registrations Almost Twice Figures of Two Years Ago

RIVERSIDE, Oct. 12.—More than 27,000 Riverside county residents will be eligible to cast votes in the November 6 Presidential and State election, it was announced by County Clerk Clayton today.

The total combined county and city registration as the election rolls closed the evening of October 6, was 27,729, nearly double the electoral enrollment of two years ago, it was disclosed. New registrants since the August primaries number 3730, while hundreds of transfers have added to the duties of the clerk's force.

Republicans maintain their dominance in the county with a ratio of practically three to one, the statistics show. Persons specifying affiliation with the G.O.P. totaled 20,992 for both city and county while the Democrats are 6554 in number. The "decline to state" column offers opportunities for both the leading parties to enrich their rolls as there were 1304 persons who did not designate any party attachment.

Judge Congden Dies at Home in Pasadena

PASADENA, Oct. 12. — Roscoe Paul Congden, who resided in this city for fifteen years and served several terms as local police judge, died yesterday at his home, 2722 Kenwood avenue, Los Angeles.

Judge Congden, who in recent years maintained offices in the Wilcox Building, Los Angeles, came to Pasadena in 1897. He studied law in the office of Judge J. H. Merriam and was admitted to the bar in 1900.

He is a former Master of Pasadena Masonic Lodge, No. 272, and was formerly Worthy Patron of Pasadena Chapter, No. 108, O.E.S.

Besides his widow, Mrs. Grace E. Congden, he leaves two daughters ...

Memorial Fund for Policeman

MONROVIA, Oct. 12.—Members of Odd Fellows lodge in conjunction with the local police department are joining forces in raising a memorial fund for the family of Massie E. Morris, veteran police officer, who was killed last Friday ...

Creator Tries Again

Above is the mystery monoplane taking off from Mahoney Airport at San Diego. Details of construction have been carefully guarded but revolutionary features may be seen in the low wing and wide landing-gear tread. Below is Donald A. Hall, designer of the craft that Lindbergh flew to Paris, who conceived this new ship.

BIRD REFUGE MAY BECOME SCENIC SPOT

Bids for Improvement Give Reason for Expecting More Than Planned at First

SANTA BARBARA, Oct. 12.—The bird refuge at the entrance to the city for which Mrs. W. A. Clark, widow of former Senator Clark of Montana, gave $50,000 to improve, can be transformed into a scenic lagoon for approximately $29,000, it was revealed today following the opening of bids for its improvement by the City Council.

The R. L. Oakley Company of Palo Alto bid $28,453 for the work, indicating, City Engineer Brown said, that nearly twice the contemplated work could be done with Mrs. Clark's gift. The highest bid was submitted by the Western Dredging Company of Los Angeles, which submitted a figure of $99,616. The engineer's estimate was $56,000.

Specifications call for the dredging of the entire pond and the raising of two islands in the center. On the shore will be laid pedestrian and bridle paths, with suitable shrubbery planted around the thirty-acre refuge.

House Robbed as Family Visits ...

W.C.T.U. FOR WILLEBRANDT

State Convention Indorses Stand of Official

Group Assails Smith in Action for Hoover

Numerous Strong Resolutions Passed by Body

REDLANDS, Oct. 12. — Entire confidence in Mrs. Mabel Walker Willebrandt and an unqualified pledge to support Herbert Hoover for President feature the resolutions adopted by the State W.C.T.U. convention here today, after the report made by the committee of which Dr. Nora T. McNeil was chairman.

The Willebrandt resolution commended her energetic demand for enforcement of the prohibition law and took great satisfaction in "the honest and straightforward speeches which she is making during the campaign." The Hoover resolution said:

SMITH AVOIDED

"Realizing that no official unless he believes in a law will faithfully enforce it, we pledge ourselves to vote for Hoover, the dry candidate."

The convention also adopted a resolution to support Initiative Measure No. 5 to repeal the boxing and wrestling law. Another demanded that judges and prohibition officers be more considerate for the safety of the public in granting probation privileges to violators of the Eighteenth Amendment. Another adopted, contained the slogan for the coming year, "The protection of our youth from the determined efforts of the cigarette trust to enslave them and an unalterable stand opposed to the smoking of cigarettes by girls and women."

A resolution supporting efforts of Imperial county to get a prohibition agent to watch young people crossing the border at Mexicali. Another urged a more determined effort than ever to bring to the attention of people the harmful effects of alcohol. Anther struck at the sale of medical wine tonics. Another commended the State Department of Education for placing child study as a part of its program of adult education under high schools.

Prediction that Herbert Hoover will win an overwhelming victory in November and a brief outline of the part that Hoover played in the passage of the Eighteenth Amendment were given in an address this afternoon by Virgil G. Hinshaw, for twelve years chairman of the Prohibition National Committee. He said:

HOOVER GAVE IDEA

"I might say that I intend to vote for Hoover, for three reasons: I like his sentiments, I like his ability and I like his background. He was raised a Quaker in Iowa. His mother was a member of the W.C.T.U., and a Holiness preacher. His Uncle John Y. Hoover, was our pastor in Pleasant Plane, Iowa, for some years.

"I met Hoover for about sixty seconds, in 1918, when I was in Washington. I had called on Congressman Charles H. Randall to inquire about the prospect of securing War Prohibition. Randall said for us to get the argument in the newspapers and have the people send letters and telegrams to their congressman. I then went to see Hoover, the Food Commissioner. He said, 'The thing to do is to get a page of prohibition facts and argument in one thousand newspapers and wipe the whole damnable liquor traffic out overnight.' We took the message to John M. Patterson, head of the National Cash Register Company, a wonderful character who employed 7000 men and was giving away $500,000 per year. Patterson said, 'I will pay the advertising bill.' He then sat down and helped to prepare the material, and paid for 1500 newspaper plates which were sent to 1500 newspapers over the country, and prohibition facts and argument were circulated to that extent as a result of the suggestion of Herbert Hoover and Charles H. Randall. Randall thereafter introduced his war prohibition measure.

. f . **(left)** This article, published in "Popular Science Monthly," clearly describes Hall's accomplishments in developing the Hall X-1, which could have a load placed anywhere in the plane without affecting its stability, safety, or performance. These were the revolutionary benefits of this tandem wing design. **(right)** Once the Hall X-1 had been built and tested, Hall received a lot of press. He had already begun several commercial and high-performance designs, which were equally well received. *Provided by the estate of Donald A. Hall, Sr.*

A WIZARD OF THE AIR LANES

Donald A. Hall, Former Central Member, Not Satisfied with Having Designed Lindbergh's "Spirit of St. Louis," Now Turns to Perfecting an Economical Plane That Flies Itself

By PAUL E. LOCKWOOD

My best regards to the members of Brooklyn Central — my home town Y.

Donald Hall

AS he flies through the trackless wastes of the skies, does Col. Charles Lindbergh's fancy ever turn to the contraption of wood, metal and canvas which holds him suspended halfway between the earth and the stars? One loose bolt, one inaccurate calculation in working out a stress, one were insufficient to stand the strain thrust upon it by the throbbing machine, is enough. The slim young Viking who is now the beau ideal of the civilized world would share the fate of that adventurous, fair youth of Greek fable, Icarus.

They used to tell in ancient Icaria of how Minos, King of Crete, imprisoned Daedalus, the greatest inventor of the age. Daedalus had contrived the Labyrinth, in which the King had confined the monster, Minotaur. Then he had fallen into the king's disfavor. Sharing his father's imprisonment was Icarus, slim and daring son of the scientist. Daedalus's genius turned toward escape. He contrived two marvelous sets of wings, from feathers, thread and wax, which were fastened to the back behind the shoulder blades. After practicing flight and teaching his son the intricacies of the wings, he offered a bit of fatherly advice. Let Ovid, first poet of the Augustinian age, tell it in his stately metre:

"My Icarus! I warn thee fly
Along the middle track: not low,
not high:
If low, thy plumes
may flag with
ocean's spray:

"RECEIVING THE COLONEL'S HANDIWRITING"

Donald Hall is seen at the right end of the line being congratulated by Col. Lindbergh on the success of "The Spirit of St. Louis."

Page Twelve

If high, the sun may dart his fiery ray."

They flew. The dungeon walls were impotent against the first flight of man. Straight over the sea they soared happily, the son following his father. The sheer joy of flying, the exultation of escape, made the lad more venturesome. His father's instruction became a dim memory as he winged his way higher and higher toward the sun. The blazing solar rays melted the wax which bound the feathers into the wings. The wings disintegrated, and the tragic youth fell like a plummet into the sea that far below glittered in the sunlight.

What a perfect analogy could have been drawn between the ill-starred Icarus and Col. Lindbergh, had the latter's plane been of such frail stuff as those Grecian plumes. Suppose the North Atlantic sun had melted some glue in the wings, suppose that an ice coating on the plane had proved too much for part of the steering apparatus. It would have been just another lost plane and the slim pilot would have joined that great company which began so long ago in the Aegean.

The fact remains that neither sleet nor sun could stop the "Spirit of St.

BESIDE HIS NEWEST INVENTION

Mr. Hall has just perfected a small, low-wing monoplane which has flown long distances in California with the controls free

Louis." Modern science proved itself superior to the genius of Greek mythology. A Brooklyn engineer designed this perfect plane, which now rests for the ages in the Smithsonian Institution, Washington, D. C., succeeded where Daedalus failed. He is the silent partner of the famous "We" firm—Donald A. Hall of Brooklyn, a former member of Central Y. M. C. A. and a graduate of Pratt Institute of Technology, this hero. He has been residing, while in California, at the San Diego "Y."

This slim young man is one of the mechanical wizards of aviation. There were a few intimate associates of his who believed as much before Lindbergh's flights. That epic deed reaffirmed their belief in Hall and inculcated it into millions of others. As if to prove his status as a wizard, Hall has now electrified the aviation industry by revealing his newest invention, a low wing monoplane which will practically fly itself. The pilot may freely remove his hands from the controls, as the accompanying photograph reveals. The plane has flown itself for long stretches on the Pacific Coast.

Let Mr. Hall tell in his own words how he came to build Lindbergh's deathless plane. He recently wrote to the Pratt alumni, thus:

"On February 26, 1927, Colonel Charles A. Lindbergh (then Captain) arrived in San Diego for the purpose of setting forth to the Ryan Airlines his ideas on securing a plane in which he might successfully compete for the Orteig prize for the first New York to Paris flight. A conference attended by Colonel Lindbergh, Mr. B. Franklin Mahoney,

President of the Ryan Airlines, and the writer was at once held, and plans were formulated for designing a monoplane which could make such a flight.

"There were a number of unusual problems to be met in designing a plane of the characteristics possessed by the 'Spirit of St. Louis.' Perhaps the first and most important of these unusual considerations was that of a good power reserve on takeoff, and it was this that caused considerable thought, although after careful consideration this problem was adequately met, as will hereinafter be set forth. The other problems of design which are novel are (1) those of locating the pilot to a point of maximum safety; (2) that of providing sufficient space for a gasoline capacity for a 3,600 mile flight; (3) that of providing a landing gear which would be capable of withstanding the strains and stresses occasioned by both taking off and landing with full load; (4) that of designing a structure capable of supporting the unusually heavy load with a sufficient load factor; and many other minor details which the writer will not endeavor to discuss.

Page Thirteen

"Unusually large wings for this size airplane are provided to derive sufficient lift to carry the heavy load and to give sufficient power reserve, since, in general, the lifting power is directly proportional to the wing area of the plane. At the start of the New York to Paris flight the wing loading was 16.5 lbs. per sq. ft., which is, of course, the weight of the airplane per square foot of wing surface.

"To meet Colonel Lindbergh's requirement of safety for the pilot, the main or central gasoline tank is located forward of the pilot's cabin. Directly to the rear of the motor is a 25 gallon oil tank which provides an excellent fire-wall to protect the fuselage gasoline tanks, which are directly aft therefrom, from fire hazard, and the pilot is thus placed in a position of maximum safety from possible injury due to being crushed by gasoline tanks in case of any possible landing accident.

"The gasoline tanks are composed of a forward tank of 88 gallon capacity (above described) located behind the oil tank, and to the rear of this tank is the main or central tank of 210 gallon capacity. In the wing structure are three tanks with a total capacity of 152 gallons. All tanks connect with a Lunkenheimer distributor in the pilot's cabin which distributes fuel from any tank to the carburetor, and it is also possible to pump gasoline from any one tank to any other tank. Connecting with the engine are two separate fuel systems for safety in case of stoppage or a leak in any one system.

"The landing gear shock absorber unit is of a type which internally resembles a trombone, and uses a shock absorber cord of eight individual links with 6½ inches rise. The landing gear axles together with the tail skid, are made of chrome molybdenum steel tubing heat treated to 180,000 lbs. per sq. in. and capable of withstanding four times the full gross weight of the plane.

"For covering, the cowl or nose portion is sheet aluminum (0.049" thick) and the fuselage and wings are each covered with grade "A" cotton treated with a preparation of cellulose acetate

which provides considerable strengthening."

Col. Lindbergh and the former Central member worked side by side in the drafting rooms in Los Angeles before the momentous flight. One was tackling the problems of aerial navigation, the solving of which was to win him the Orteig prize. The other was designing the plane to win the prize. What does the intrepid flying Colonel think of his co-worker, you ask? Here is an extract from report of reception by Aeronautical Chamber of Commerce, at the Waldorf-Astoria, in the N. Y. Times, June 17, 1927.

"Colonel Lindbergh then gave another illustration of his modesty and desire to give full credit to others, which have marked him since he became famous, by referring to Donald Hall, designer of his plane.

"'There is one person to whom great credit belongs,' he continued. 'He is Donald Hall. I am going to ask him to rise so that you may see another one of the partnership, we.'

"Mr. Hall, a slender young man, arose with a smile blushing. Enthusiastic applause greeted him."

So Central members, for many years hence, will watch with eager eyes the career of this former member, whose brilliant engineering career seems but an introduction to greater conquests to come.

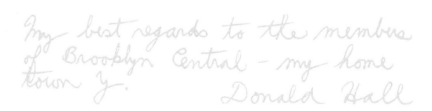

"LINDY" AND "DON"

For three months, this pair worked beside each other in the drafting room, one perfecting a plane and the other calculating on charts his chance of eternal fame.

Page Fourteen

. g . An article published by Brooklyn Central, Hall's hometown YMCA.
Provided by the estate of Donald A. Hall, Sr.

My best regards to the members of Brooklyn Central — my home town Y.

Donald Hall

. i .

. h .

. j .

. h . Newlyweds Elizabeth and Donald Hall.

. i . Hall and his wife spent a lot of time at the beach.

. j . Donald Hall and Elizabeth Walker married during the Christmas holidays in 1933. Their only son was born in November of 1934. After Hall joined Consolidated Aircraft in 1935, he and Elizabeth, who was a school teacher, built their new home in Point Loma, a suburb of San Diego. This picture was taken on their honeymoon in Santa Barbara in 1933.

. k . Donald Hall and his only son, Don Hall, Jr.

. l . Don Hall, Jr., at four years old.

(. h . - . l .) Provided by the estate of Donald A. Hall, Sr.

. k .

. l .

U.S. Naval Air Station, North Island
San Diego, California

Donald A. Hall

Farewell and Good Luck. Your fine contribution to the progress of North Island is recognized and appreciated. We, your friends, wish for you health, happiness, and continued achievement in the years ahead.

OVERHAUL & REPAIR DEPARTMENT

. **m** . Hall is pictured in his office at North Island Naval Air Station just before his retirement. Hall was head supervisor for the North Island Helicopter Engineering branch until he retired in 1963.

. **n** . When he retired from North Island, Hall was honored with this special achievement award, signed by over 100 engineers and employees working at the Navy facility.

(. m . & . n .) Provided by the estate of Donald A. Hall, Sr.

. o . **(opposite page)** Donald A. Hall served as technical advisor for the 1957 motion picture "Spirit of St. Louis," starring Jimmy Stewart. *Provided by the estate of Donald A. Hall, Sr.*

. p . Hall's technical notes for the motion picture. *Courtesy of the Karpeles Museum.*

. p .

149

. q .

. q . In the 1950's, only 50 years after the first flight by the Wright brothers at Kitty Hawk, Donald Hall was presented with a Pioneer Aviation Award. General Doolittle of the World War II Tokyo Raiders fame, along with several local San Diego dignitaries, signed the certificate.

. r . The 40th Anniversary of the *Spirit's* flight was celebrated at North Island in 1967, one year before Hall passed away. The airplane is a replica of the *Spirit,* built by Tallman Aviation. Later, this replica was lost in a museum fire.

(. q . & . r .) Provided by the estate of Donald A. Hall, Sr.

. r .

Left to Right: John Van Der Linde, Donald Hall, Harold Von Brieson, T. Claude Ryan and Carl Hatfield.

. s . At the 40th anniversary celebration on North Island, Donald Hall and an official from their local AIAA chapter have their photo taken.

. t . Commemorative announcement for the 40th anniversary of Charles Lindbergh's flight to St. Louis and, eventually, Paris.

(. s . & . t .) Provided by the estate of Donald A. Hall, Sr.

. **u** . Examples of correspondence from Charles Lindbergh to Donald A. Hall, Sr. over the many years of their friendship. *Provided by the estate of Donald A. Hall, Sr*

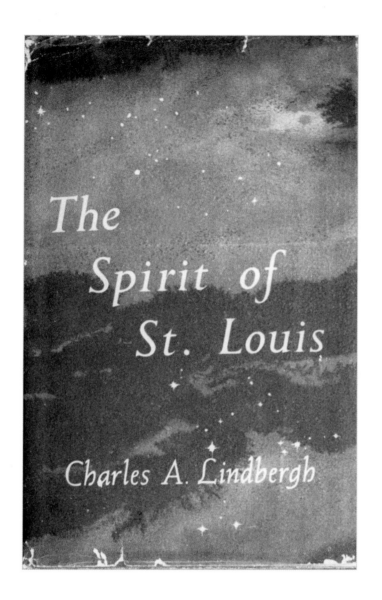

. v . **(left)** This photograph depicts the rare first draft cover for the Pulitzer Prize winning book, "The Spirit of St. Louis." Hall was given this pre-press copy before the book's 1953 publication date. Hall and his son, Don Hall, Jr., worked together to prepare the technical appendix for the book. **(right)** Lindbergh inscribed this copy of "The Spirit of St. Louis" with a note to Donald Hall, his friend and collaborator. The inscription reads, "To Donald A. Hall, who had such a great part in the flight of the Spirit of St. Louis." It's signed "Charles A Lindbergh, August 1953." The book was published on September 14 of that year. Hall prepared the sections of the appendix pertaining to the *Spirit's* performance flight data, how the aircraft was designed, and how it was built. Don Hall, Jr. prepared the drawings of the *Spirit of St. Louis. Provided by the estate of Donald. A. Hall, Sr.*

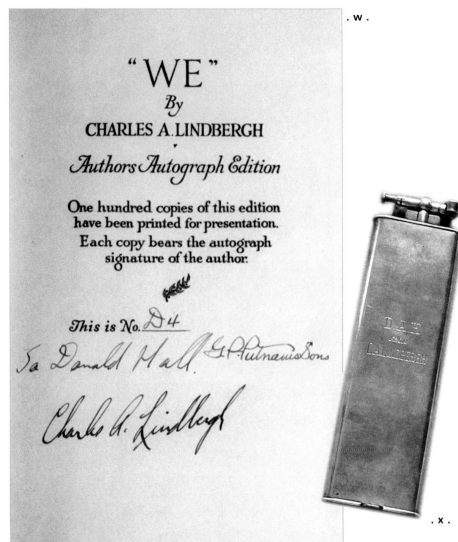

"WE"

By

CHARLES A. LINDBERGH

·

Authors Autograph Edition

One hundred copies of this edition
have been printed for presentation.
Each copy bears the autograph
signature of the author.

This is No. D4

To Donald Hall. G.P.Putnams Sons

Charles A. Lindbergh

. x .

. w . This specially prepared limited edition of "We" was presented by Lindbergh to Hall. Only 100 copies were printed. Hall had reviewed an earlier edition of "We," which he edited in 1927. The changes he made were included in this edition. Lindbergh specifically designated this book for Hall out of the 100 copies printed of the limited edition. Notice the addition of a "D" before the number 4. Lindbergh also inscribed the book, "To Donald Hall". The publisher signed it, as well.

. x . Charles Lindbergh had this special sterling silver table lighter made for his friend, Donald Hall. The lighter is engraved, "D.A.H. from C.A. Lindbergh."

. y . [opposite page] Charles Lindbergh was a pilot's pilot, pushing the envelope for aviation. Donald Hall was an engineer's engineer, always inventing and innovating to achieve a complex goal or task. Together the two young men, ages 25 and 28, did the impossible with their 60-day miracle creation. *Charles Lindbergh was the "Spirit," while Donald Hall was the "Creator."*

(. w . - . y .) Provided by the estate of Donald A. Hall, Sr.

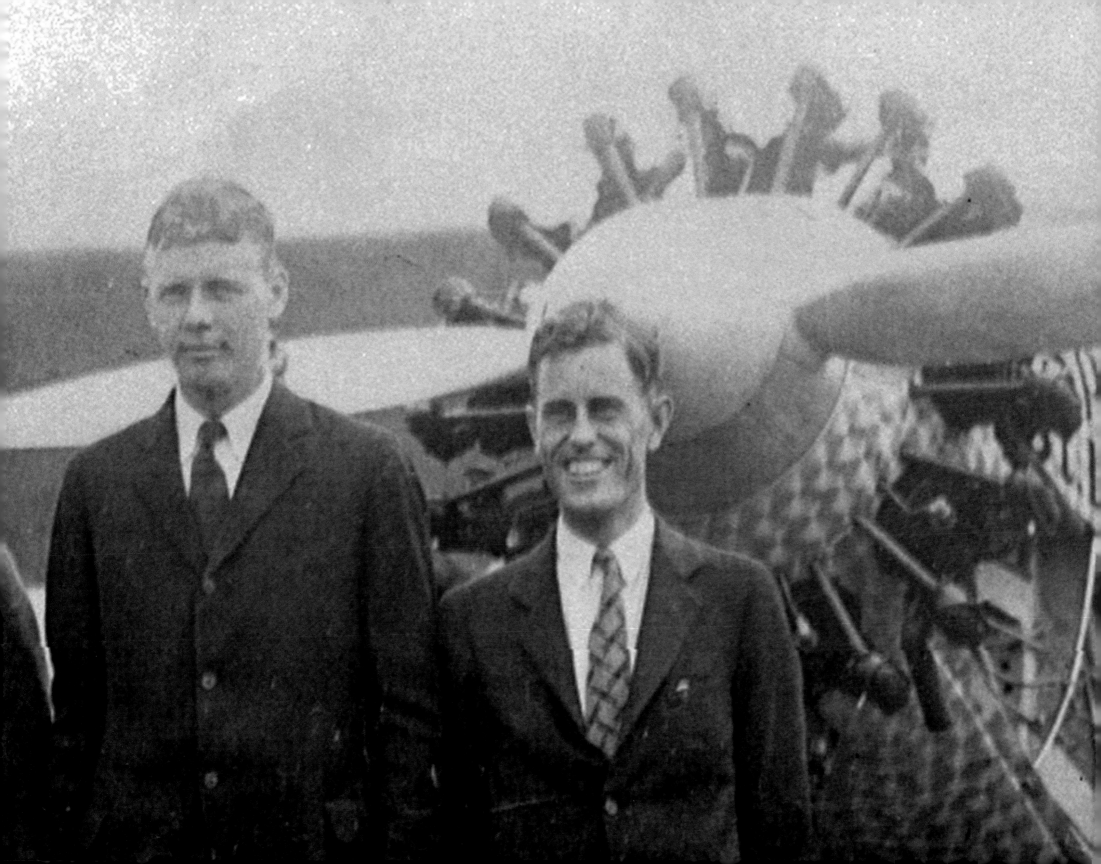

National Aviation Hall of Fame (http://www.nationalaviation.org)
National Museum of Naval Aviation (http://www.naval-air.org)
Pratt Institute (http://www.pratt.edu)
San Diego Air & Space Museum (http://www.aerospacemuseum.org)
EAA Air Venture Museum (http://www.airventuremuseum.org)
September 11th Memorial Project (http://www.spiritofamericafoundation.org)
Smithsonian Institution (http://www.si.edu)
Smithsonian National Air & Space Museum (http://www.nasm.edu)
The Cradle of Aviation Museum (http://www.cradleofaviation.org)
Yale University (http://www.yale.edu)

FLIGHT/AVIATION

AIAA Evolution of Flight Campaign (http://www.flight100.org)
Aircraft Owners and Pilots Association (http://www.aopa.org)
*American Institute of Aeronautics and Astronautics (AIAA) (http://www.aiaa.org)
Centennial of Flight Commission (http://www.centennialofflight.gov)
Fantasy of Flight (http://fantasyofflight.com)
Jane's Aerospace (http://www.janes.com/aerospace)
NASA's Aero-Space Technology (http://www.aero-space.nasa.gov)
National Air and Space Administration (NASA) (http://www.nasa.gov)
Orbital Air, Inc. (http://www.orbitalair.com)
The Federal Aviation Administration (FAA) (http://www.faa.gov)
The X-Prize Foundation (http://www.xprize.org)

AERONAUTICAL ENGINEERING/DESIGN

"Aviation Internet Directory: Best 500 Aviation Websites" — McGraw-Hill Publication
Edinburgh Engineering Virtual Library (http://www.eevl.ac.uk)
Embry Riddle Aeronautical University (ERAU) (http://www.erau.edu)
ERAU Virtual Library (http://www.embryriddle.edu/libraries/virtual/)
Library of Congress (http://www.loc.com)
NASA Quest: Learn Aerospace Online (http://quest.arc.nasa.gov/aero/)

Popular Mechanics (http://www.popularmechanics.com)

Scientific American (http://www.sciam.com)

***The Society of Automotive Engineers (SAE)** (http://www.sae.org/aeromag)

ENGINEERING BOOKS:

"Birdflight as The Basis of Aviation" by Otto Lilienthal (the book that inspired the Wright Brothers and, thus, all modern aviation)

"The Papers of Wilbur and Orville Wright: Including the Chanute-Wright Letters" by Wilbur and Orville Wright (two-volume set)

HELICOPTER/GYRO-CRAFT DESIGN

American Helicopter Museum (http://www.helicoptermuseum.org)

***American Helicopter Society** (http://www.vtol.org)

Helicopter Association International (http://www.rotor.com)

Helicopter Museum (http://www.helicoptermuseum.co.uk)

Whirly Girls: International Women Helicopter Pilots (http://www.whirlygirls.org)

* Groups/organizations Donald Hall was involved with during his career

REFERENCES

"A Visit with the Spirit of St. Louis Designer" — The AIAA Tabloid, San Diego Section of the American Institute of Aeronautics & Astronautics (MAY 1967).

"A Wizard of the Air Lanes" — Brooklyn Central.

"Aviation Quests for Greater Safety - New Plane Has Radical Features" — New York Times (JANUARY 20, 1929).

"Brooklyn Boy Designed Lindbergh's Airplane" — Brooklyn Sunday Eagle (MAY 22, 1927).

"Brooklyn Boy — The Designer of NYP Plane" — Brooklyn Times (MAY 22, 1927).

"Designing the Spirit of St. Louis" by Donald A. Hall — Pratt Tech News (JULY 1927).

"Hall Designs New Airplane" — Los Angeles Times (OCTOBER 13, 1928).

"Hall's Mother is Happy" — New York Sunday Times (MAY 22, 1927).

"How Hall Designed Plane" — Brooklyn Eagle (JULY 10, 1927).

"Lindbergh Arrives on Record-Breaking Flight" — New York Herald, European Edition - Paris (MAY 22, 1927).

"Lindbergh Souvenir Number" — Mid-week Pictorial, The New York Times, Co. (JUNE 23, 1927 - VOL. XXV, NO. 18).

"Lindbergh's Full Story" — Transocean Flights Current History, The New York Times Co. (JULY 1927 - VOL. XXVI, NO. 4).

"Lindbergh's Trans-Atlantic Flight" — Aviation Stories and Mechanics (JULY 1927 - VOL. 1, NO. 1).

"Mathematics & Maps Made Lindbergh's Flight Possible" — San Diego Sun (MAY 23, 1927).

"Men and Ideas Setting the Pace in Aviation" — Popular Science Monthly (FEBRUARY 1929).

"Plane Used by Lindbergh is Stock Model" — New York Evening Journal (MAY 23, 1927).

"Radical Changes Seen in Hall Monoplane" — Los Angeles Times (OCTOBER 13, 1928).

"Ryan NYP — A Development of the Ryan M-2" — Aviation (JUNE 20, 1927).

"Ryan NYP, Spirit of St. Louis" — Aero Digest (MAY 1952).

"San Diego's Paris 'Hop' Hope" — The San Diego Sun (MAY 21, 1927).

"Son of Brooklynite Designed Lindbergh NYP Plane" — Standard Union (MAY 22, 1927).

"Technical Preparation of the Ryan New York-Paris Airplane" by Donald A. Hall — Aero Digest (JULY 1927).

"The Spirit of St. Louis" by Donald A. Hall — Flight Magazine (JUNE 9, 1927 - VOL. XIX, NO. 23).

"Victorious Plane Originated by Brooklyn Man" — New York American (MAY 23, 1927).

ADDENDUM

AFTER READING SPIRIT AND CREATOR, THERE MAY BE SOME LINGERING QUESTIONS. Perhaps you wondered how the records from the creation of the *Spirit of St. Louis* came to be in the trunk that my son Nova discovered in our garage nearly 75 years later. The short answer is that I put them there.

My mother passed away in 1972, four years after my father's death. I kept their house in Point Loma for a number of years before selling it. During those years, I organized many vital and critical documents, including my father's records and keepsakes from his extensive career in aircraft design and engineering. I sorted through several large file cabinets and stored many of the materials pertaining to the *Spirit of St. Louis* in an old steamer trunk that I believe my father obtained in the early 1930's. Other assorted items were stored in boxes. I moved the trunk and the boxes to my home in Idylwild, in the San Jacinto mountains, where Nova was born. Over the years, I continued to cart my father's trunk and boxes around during each move.

That explains how the items got there, but how did these treasures remain hidden for so long? Well, some of them didn't. A few boxes were opened over the years and an item or two joined the rest of our family's personal effects. Nova even played with some of them as a child, and I gave him my father's silver lighter in his mid-teens. But most of them were simply forgotten.

I spent several years as an engineer, first for Ryan Aeronautics where I worked on a vertical takeoff test bed design. Then, for four years, I was employed by Convair Astronautics. There, I worked in the Atlas Missile program under the supervision of Kraft Eriche, who had been recruited from Germany after the war. I quit Convair to set up a computer center, the first large scale Scientific Service Bureau in San Diego. Among our clients were the Naval Electronics Laboratory and Rohr Corporation. The business was ultimately sold to Cubic Corporation.

By the time we moved to Idylwild, I had left my engineering

career behind to pursue other goals, and my herb business occupied all of my attention. I had neither the time nor the inclination to go through my father's things again, so when Nova started to take an interest in his grandfather in his late teens, I freely passed on everything that was formerly my father's. The trunk was not noticed, however, and was shoved to the back of the garage where it remained, forgotten, until Nova found it in 1999.

While Nova had long been aware that his grandfather had designed the *Spirit of St. Louis*, discovering the old trunk made the historical event come alive for him. He wanted to know more, not only about Donald Hall, the aeronautical engineer who designed the *Spirit of St. Louis*, but especially about Donald Hall, the man. That's when the idea for this book was born.

As Nova uncovered the past, I began to remember things I hadn't thought about for years. I remembered not only the events of my childhood and teen years, but the numerous discussions I had with my father. We talked of many things and, certainly, the key role he played in building the *Spirit of St. Louis* was one of the topics. He was very proud to have been a part of that historic event. But, as much as he had enjoyed the design and building of the *Spirit*, some of what happened after that event troubled my father.

The ensuing publicity especially concerned him. My father was a man of integrity and high principles. Both as an engineer and as an individual, facts were important to him and the facts pertaining to the creation of the *Spirit of St. Louis* were distorted in many ways in the years following its transatlantic flight. More than that he refused to say. "The truth will eventually come out," is what he always told me.

As Nova researched Donald Hall's life and his involvement with the *Spirit*, he became aware of several discrepancies between what had actually happened and what had been reported in the local press and in other books, as well as through exhibits at the local airplane museum. I only began to understand my father's frustration with the way some of the facts had been misrepresented when Nova showed me original documents that allowed us to clarify my father's views and position on the subject.

The distortions primarily concern three issues: (1) the extent of T. Claude Ryan's involvement with the *Spirit of St. Louis*; (2) which, if any, aircraft served as the basis for the *Spirit's* design; and (3) Charles Lindbergh's living arrangements during the creation of the *Spirit*. Was Ryan the factory manager during the *Spirit's* construction or was that role filled by Hawley Bowlus? Was the *Spirit's* design a modification of the existing Ryan M-2 or was it based on the B-1, the aircraft Donald Hall had been hired by Ryan to design and that was still in development? Did Lindbergh live with Ryan's sales manager, A.J. Edwards, or in a room in the YMCA next to my father's? Those questions are answered, to some degree, in this book.

The following is my understanding of certain events, based on conversations with my father, Donald Hall, and memories of my own experiences.

In late 1926, T. Claude Ryan, president of Ryan Airlines, was negotiating the sale of his portion of the company to his business partner, B. F. Mahoney. Ryan Airlines was sold outright to B. F. Mahoney before or at the start of the New Year. The sale included the rights to manufacture two high-wing monoplane models designed by a previous engineer who had worked for Ryan Airlines. These aircraft models included the Ryan M-1 and M-2.

When B. F. Mahoney took over Ryan Airlines in early 1927, he had to hire a new engineer, since that position was vacant. My father, Donald A. Hall, had already been working as a freelance aeronautical engineer for Ryan Airlines on the weekends, making some improvements to the current models. During the week, Donald Hall worked for the Douglas Company in Santa Monica as an aircraft designer, directly under the supervision of Donald Douglas.

Knowing of my father's interest in heading up a new production design and having witnessed my father's dedication and experience, B.F. Mahoney naturally hired him as his new chief engineer. Donald Hall joined Ryan Airlines full time in late January of 1927, just prior to the company's first telegram from Charles Lindbergh, who was inquiring about a plane to cross the Atlantic. My father had been hired to design a new Ryan Airlines model, and he had already begun work on it. Later, after the historic transatlantic flight, this model was finished. Its design incorporated many features that the *Spirit of St. Louis* had proven effective, such as the wide tread "outrigger" style landing gear. The name of this new model was the B-1 Brougham.

When he went to work for Ryan Airlines, my father didn't have the time or the need for a house, so he moved into the San Diego YMCA, a short distance from the Ryan Airlines factory. When Charles Lindbergh arrived in San Diego in February of 1927 to begin the design and construction of the *Spirit of St. Louis*, he also stayed at the YMCA, in a room next to my father's. My father was always very clear about that fact.

Soon after I was born in November of 1934 (several years after the transatlantic flight) my father began working as a group design engineer for Consolidated Aircraft. After being employed by Consolidated, he designed and helped build his new house in Point Loma on Xenophon Street. Later, the Ryan family bought a large house on the same street, about three blocks down the hill. It overlooked the Naval Training Center, Lindbergh Field airport, Ryan Aeronautical (T. Claude Ryan's new company), and Consolidated Aircraft. My father, being the practical man that he was, let my mother have the car while he walked to and from the bus stop each day, passing the Ryan home on the way.

As I got older, I played with a number of the Ryan children, even though I remembered my father saying there was something going on between him and T. Claude Ryan. He wouldn't talk to me about it, since it was quite complicated. I also met Sandy Fleet, one of Ruebin Fleet's children. Major Fleet was the president of Consolidated Aircraft, renamed Convair after the war when it merged with Vultee Aircraft from Fort Worth, Texas.

Because of the proximity of our three families and many other important people in the San Diego area, I learned that my father never really wanted to talk about the stories and misinformation that were circulating about Lindbergh, the *Spirit of St. Louis*, and the Ryan saga.

Later, after attending San Diego State University, I went to work at Ryan Aeronautical as a junior engineer, working in the Preliminary Design section. (Ryan Aeronautical was eventually sold to Northrop Grumman and is sometimes confused with Ryan Airlines.) I also helped analyze test data from the design of future flying drones used as aircraft targets. During this time, a most peculiar event occurred. I was invited into the office of T. Claude Ryan to discuss any problems I may have had with their interpretation of Ryan's involvement with the *Spirit of St. Louis* or Lindbergh's flight. William "Bill" Wagner (Ryan's vice president and the author of "Ryan, the Aviator") was present.

I distinctly recall that they wanted me either to agree with them or argue with them about what I knew the truth to be. I did neither. I told them I didn't really have an opinion and, basically, kept my mouth shut. Although I had been given a lot of information, I didn't want to make a judgment without making sure of its accuracy. If they wanted to confirm the situation or find out what others had said, I told them they needed to talk directly to my father or Lindbergh. As far as I know, they never did.

My only direct connection to the *Spirit* occurred when Charles Lindbergh was writing *"The Spirit of St. Louis."* He asked my father to provide several technical drawings and an engineering data section, later published in the book's appendix. Because my father was so busy at the time and because I had a special talent for drafting and for the inking process, he asked me to help. So I prepared three drawings of the *Spirit* on white linen and inked them. I have always felt honored that these drawings later appeared in Lindbergh's book as the three views of the *Spirit of St. Louis.*

The people who were directly involved in the *Spirit's* creation have all passed away, and it's left to those of us who remain behind to sort out the various versions of the truth. With the passage of 75 years, some issues may never be fully addressed. However, this book takes one step toward setting the record straight on behalf of my father and the other men and women who labored so intensively to build the *Spirit of St. Louis.* Through SPIRIT AND CREATOR, my father's prediction is coming to pass. The truth has, indeed, begun to come out.

DON A. HALL, JR.

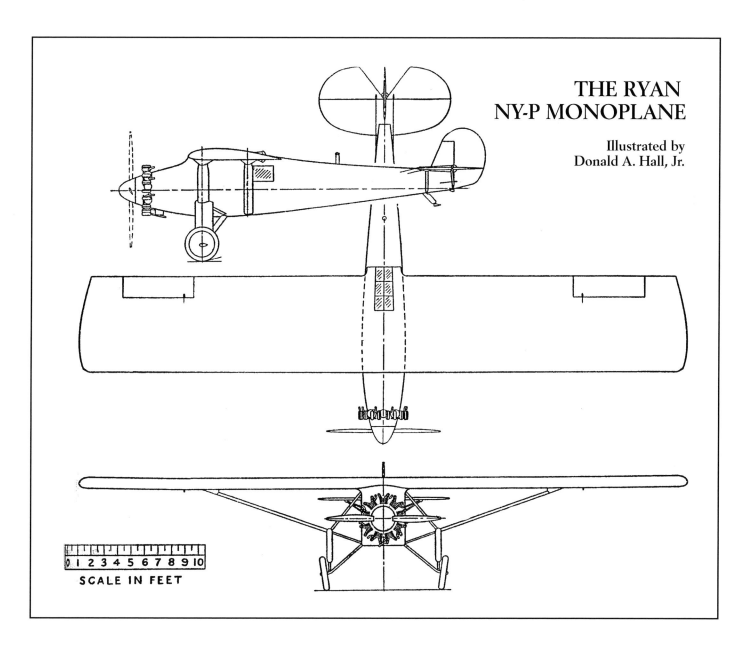

THE RYAN
NY-P MONOPLANE

Illustrated by
Donald A. Hall, Jr.

0 1 2 3 4 5 6 7 8 9 10
SCALE IN FEET

The Ryan NY-P Monoplane, *Spirit of St. Louis*. Illustrated by Donald Hall, Jr. for technical publication in *"The Spirit of St. Louis,"* written by Charles Lindbergh (1953). *Provided by the estate of Donald A. Hall, Sr.*

APPENDIX

ENGINEERING DATA ON THE *Spirit of St. Louis* — by Donald A. Hall, Chief Engineer of Ryan Airlines, Inc. (1927)
ILLUSTRATIONS OF THE *Spirit of St. Louis* — by Donald A. Hall, Jr.

These data are compiled from or based on original records, some of which are in Technical Note No. 257 of the National Advisory Committee for Aeronautics, Washington, D.C., July 1927, entitled "Technical Preparation of the Airplane, *Spirit of St. Louis,*" by Donald A Hall. The company model designation for the *Spirit of St. Louis* was "NYP" (New York-Paris).

SECTION A — DESIGN CHARACTERISTICS

GENERAL

Span	46 ft. 0 in.
Overall length	27 ft. 8 in.
Overall Height	9 ft. 10 in.
Wing cord	7 ft. 0 in.
Airfoil	Clark Y
Wing incidence	0°
Wing aspect ratio	6.6

AREAS

Wing	319.0 sq. ft.
Ailerons, each	8.0 sq. ft.
Horizontal tail	36 sq. ft.
Vertical tail	11.3 sq. ft.

POWER PLANT

Engine — Wright J-5C, "Super inspected."	
Rated power — 1800 RPM — sea level	223 BHP
Maximum power — 1950 RPM at max. air speed — sea level.	237 BHP
Propeller — duralumin — Standard Steel Propeller Co.	8 ft. 9 in. dia.
Fuel Capacity — designed	425 gal.
Main fuselage tank (under wing)	200 gal.
Nose (forward fuselage tank)	80 gal.
Three wing tanks	145 gal.
Oil capacity	25 gal.

NOTES:

RPM = engine propeller shaft speed in revolutions per minute.

BHP = brake (actual) horse power output of engine to propeller.

The capacity of the fuel tanks as built came out oversize at 210, 88, and 152 gal. respectively, totaling 450 gal.

LANDING GEAR

Tread — no load	8 ft. 9 in.
Tread — fully-deflected shock absorbers	10 ft. 0 in.
Wheel rise with fully deflected shock absorbers	8.5 in.
Tire size	30 in. x 5 in.

WEIGHTS AND LOADINGS — *(See Sec. F for weight data upon leaving New York for Paris.)*

Empty weight complete with equipment and instruments	2150 lbs.
Useful load	
Pilot	170 lb.
Miscellaneous	40 lb.
Fuel — 425 gal. Calif. gasoline at 6.12 lb./gal.	2600 lb.
Oil — 25 gal. at 7.0 lb./gal.	175 lb.
TOTAL	2985 lb.
Design gross weight, fully loaded, start of flight	3135 lb.
Lightly loaded gross weight, end of flight, without fuel and food. (10 gal. oil left)	2415 lb.
Wing loading	
Design gross weight, start of flight	16.1 lb./sq.ft.
Lightly loaded, end of flight	7.6 lb./sq.ft.
Power loading — rated	
Design gross weight, start of flight	23.0 lb./BHP
Lightly loaded, end of flight	10.8 lb./BHP

CALCULATED CENTER OF GRAVITY LOCATIONS AT SEVERAL LOADING CONDITIONS

LOADING CONDITION	GROSS WEIGHT lb.	C.G. LOCATION RELATIVE TO WING CHORD	
		LONGITUDINAL *Aft of wing leading edge*	VERTICAL *Below chord (base) line*
Design gross weight start of flight	5135	28.4%	19.2%
Normal most forward C.G. 200 gal. main tank fuel and 8 gal. oil used	3845	25.8%	15.5%
Normal most aft C.G. 10 gal. oil, food, and all fuel except 145 gal. wing fuel used	3340	*29.6%	15.2%
Lightly loaded end of flight, no fuel and food 10 gal. oil remaining	2415	27.6%	19.7%
Design gross weight without fuel, food, oil and food	2345	**29.0%	19.2%

* If the 80 gallons of fuel in the nose tank were used first, the center of gravity (C.G.) would move aft to 31.6% wing chord with a consequent reduction in the longitudinal stability. In all of his long distance flights with the NYP, Lindbergh decided to sacrifice stability to a more rearward C.G. position in case of a forced landing, thus reducing the tendency to nose over. He therefore used fuel from the nose tank before the main fuselage tank was dry.

** This C.G. location was measured by balancing the airplane in three positions (Lindbergh in the pilot's seat and miscellaneous useful load properly located). The intersection of the weight vectors located the C.G. This checked the calculated C.G. location, both longitudinal and vertical, within .15 in.

SECTION B — CALCULATED PERFORMANCE AT SEA LEVEL

Maximum Air Speed
    Design gross weight, start of flight   120 MPH
    Lightly loaded, end of flight   124.5 MPH

Minimum Air Speed
    Design gross weight, start of flight   71 MPH
    Lightly loaded, end of flight   49 MPH

Range with Zero Wind and 425 Gal. of Fuel
    Ideal economic air speeds of 97 MPH at start
      and 67 MPH at end   4110 miles
    Practical economic air speeds of 95 MPH at start
      and 75 MPH at end   4040 miles

NOTES:

MPH = miles per hour in statute miles of 5280 feet.

Maximum air speed is in level flight without the benefit of gravity in descending flight.

Minimum air speed or the stalling speed is the lowest possible speed relative to the air that an airplane is capable of flying. This is also called landing speed, but airplanes are rarely landed as slow as their minimum speeds because of the stalling danger.

Economic air speed is the speed of best fuel economy.

The conservatively calculated and measured performance figures given here for the *Spirit of St. Louis* should not be confused with the extravagant claims of performance which were often released by manufacturers of small airplanes.

SECTION C — FLIGHT TEST PERFORMANCE
MAXIMUM AIR SPEED AT SEA LEVEL

Clocked test over 3 km. Course
    (average of three runs in each direction)
    25 gal. fuel and 5 gal. oil   129 MPH

Design gross weight with 425 gal. fuel,
    developed from calculated and clocked speeds
    plotted as curves of max. speed vs. gross weight   124.5 MPH

TAKE-OFF DISTANCE

Take-off tests were made at abandoned World War I Camp Kearney, 11 miles north of the city of San Diego and .8 miles south of the present U.S. Naval Air Station, Miramar. This field, located on a Mesa, was 12,000 ft. long in the direction of the prevailing wind, had a constant downward slope of 6 ft. in 1,000 ft. toward the west, and a natural surface of hard packed clay and rock.

The take-off runs started near the east end of the field at a 485 ft. elevation. A series of seven take-off tests were made with fuel loads from 36 to 301 gal. The take-off distances were plotted against the gross weight to produce the solid line curve. The approximate take-off distance for hard ground, with zero wind, at 485 ft. elevation for 5,135 lb. design gross weight (425 gal. fuel), determined by extrapolation of the test curve was 2,250 ft.

SECTION D — NOTES ON DESIGN PROCEDURE

After intensive preliminary design analysis of aerodynamics, structures, and weights, of various configurations of the proposed airplane, it was concluded that a redesign of the production model 3-seater, open cockpit, Ryan M-2 could not make the 3,600 mile flight between New York and Paris with ample reserve fuel, and that a new design development was necessary. The short time of two months provided in the order, dated Feb. 25, 1927, which Lindbergh placed for the NYP, precluded incorporating major design features not well proven by actual service on airplanes. The next decision was to utilize as many parts of the M-2 design as practicable, to save time and cut costs.

Among major considerations involved in freezing the NYP basic design were the following:

1. *Gross Weight.* In order to carry the heavy fuel and oil load required for the proposed flight, the M-2 gross weight of 2,500 lb. had to be practically doubled in the first weight estimates.

2. *Wing.* The 36 ft. span of the M-2 had to be changed to 46 ft. to increase both the wing area (33%) and the aspect ratio for good take-off characteristics and for improved range. Fortunately the wing chord did not have to be changed, so the excellent M-2 wing rib was incorporated. Throughout the entire wing it was not possible to use any other M-2 part, due to both dimensional and structural differences.

3. *Effects of new wing on basic design.*
   a. FUSELAGE. The empennage was moved aft 24 in., which, in combination with a more forward C.G. requirement, made it necessary to move the engine forward 18 in. The 42 in. increase in fuselage structure length, in addition to the increased gross weight, prevented utilizing any M-2 fuselage part.

b. LANDING GEAR. The 6 ft 0 in. wheel tread of the M-2 (at no load) was widened to 8 ft. 9 in. to secure good ground stability with the increased wing span and doubled gross weight. The NYP landing gear design, with its fairly high wheel rise for good shock absorption, was adapted from a successful commercial single-engine transport.

4. *Empennage.* The M-2 empennage, comprising horizontal and vertical tail surfaces, was used with a minimum of change. The forward movement of the C.G. of the NYP (about 5% wing chord), combined with the 24 in. aft movement of the empennage, improved the longitudinal and directional stability, while doubling the gross weight and enlarging the wing reduced both. It was anticipated that the resulting stability would be ample for the take-off at New York and the flight across the Atlantic, but not for commercial purposes.

5. *Power Plant Installation.* The fuel and oil systems obviously could not use any of the M-2 design. The M-2 fuel system was approximately 50 gal., while the NYP was designed to carry 750% more fuel.

FINAL CONFIGURATION

The final configuration of this strut-braced high-wing monoplane was a composite of the best design features of successful military and commercial airplanes.

SECTION E — TYPICAL FEATURES

Wing. The I-section spars were made of spruce, comprising four flange members casein glued to web members. The wood ribs utilized the Warren-truss principal. Drag bracing comprised double piano wire, with compression ribs made by reinforcing standard ribs with spruce compression members. Relatively small ailerons (20% less area than on the M-2) were located 38 in. inboard of the wing tips, to avoid wing structural loads in the full load condition. The lateral control with these ailerons proved to be ample. The external struts used to brace the wing were SAE 1020 mild carbon steel tubes, streamlined with balsa wood.

Fuselage. The fuselage was built with SAE 1020 mild carbon steel tubes, welded together to form horizontal and vertical trusses.

Empennage. The vertical and horizontal surfaces were made of SAE 1020 mild carbon steel tubes to form structure and ribs. The horizontal stabilizer was adjustable from the cockpit for maintaining longitudinal balance (trim) in flight at any speed or loading condition.

Landing gear. Wide tread-split axle type. Each of the dual axles, as well as the tail skid, were made of chrome molybdenum (SAE 4130) steel tubes heat-treated to 180,000 lb. per sq. in. and streamlined with balsa wood. The "trombone" type of shock absorber utilized shock absorber cord of eight individual links in tension to give 6 1/2 in. compressive deflection of the unit.

Power Plant Installation. The oil tank, located immediately behind the engine, filled practically the entire fuselage cross section, to perform effectively the additional function of a firewall. The fuel and oil tanks were made of soft sheet steel called "ternplate," to reduce the danger of leaks developing from vibration. Each of the five fuel tanks was connected to a distribution system in the cockpit, so that fuel could be transferred by hand pumping from any tank to any other tank. Two independent fuel lines ran from the cockpit distribution system to the engine. In case the engine fuel pump in one line failed, fuel could be hand wobble-pumped from either of the fuselage tanks to one of the wing tanks, where it could then flow to the engine by gravity. The cowling and propeller spinner were made of soft aluminum. The duralumin propeller blades, which were adjustable on the ground, were set at 16 1/4° pitch.

Covering. The wing, empennage, fuselage, external struts, axles, and tail skid were covered with Grade A cotton fabric with cellulose acetate dope.

Streamlining. In relation to standard practices of the period, unusual emphasis was placed on streamlining the *Spirit of St. Louis*. As a result, in the lightly loaded condition, the maximum speed obtained was about 10 MPH higher than the maximum speed of the Ryan M-2, with the same engine, while the minimum air speed was about 8 MPH lower than that of the M-2.

1. The accuracy of the airfoil contour of the wing was increased by:
   a. Wing ribs spaced 11 in. apart instead of the conventional 14 to 15 in.
   b. Plywood completely around the leading edge of the front spar.
   c. Wing tips formed of balsa wood planking with the airfoil contour in plan and faired spanwise sections.

2. At the juncture of external struts with wing, fuselage, horizontal stabilizer, etc., aluminum fairings were made to enclose strut ends and fittings to reduce the interferential resistance.

3. Each landing gear shock absorber unit was covered by a stream lined aluminum enclosure. The wheels were streamlined with doped fabric laced to the tires at their maximum width.

4. The engine and forward fuselage cowling were carefully faired into the remainder of the fuselage.

Safety of pilot's location. The location of the pilot behind the main fuel tank, as well as all the other tanks, had the following advantages:

1. The pilot could not be crushed by the weight of the tank and fuel in a crack-up.

2. The C.G. of the design fuel load was close to the airplane C.G. for improved longitudinal stability in the critical first part of the flight.

177

**SECTION F — CHARACTERISTICS OF THE *Spirit of St. Louis*
UPON LEAVING NEW YORK FOR PARIS**

WEIGHTS

Summary

Empty, complete with equipment and instruments   2,150 lb.
Useful load
    Pilot   170 lb.
    Miscellaneous   40 lb.
    *Fuel, 450 gal. (actual)   2,750 lb.
    Oil 20 gal.   140 lb.
    TOTAL   3,100 lb.

Gross weight fully loaded 5,250 lb.
*At New York, Lindbergh decided to exceed the design fuel
load by completely filling all tanks (see Sec. A).

Equivalent net weight empty

Assume that a fuel capacity of 60 gal. and an oil
capacity of 5 gal. is sufficient for ordinary flying.
Then the weight of excess tanks, special equipment,
and special instruments not required in ordinary
flying is   450 lb.

Equivalent net weight empty
(2,150 minus 450)   1,700 lb.

Weight efficiency

Equivalent useful load (5,250 minus 1700)   3,550 lb.
Ratio of equivalent useful load
    to equivalent weight empty   2.1
Ratio of gross weight to equivalent weight empty   3.1

LOADINGS

Wing loading   16.5 lb./sq. ft
Power loading, rated   23.6 lb./BHP

MINIMUM STRUCTURAL LOAD FACTORS
(5,250 LB. Gross Weight)

Wing structure in high incidence condition   3.3
Wing structure in low incidence condition   2.3
Landing gear in three point landing condition   4.0

CALCULATED PERFORMANCE AT SEA LEVEL
WITH 450 GAL. FUEL *(Based on calculated performance of Sec. B)*

Maximum air speed   119.5 MPH
Minimum air speed   72 MPH
Range at economic air speeds with zero wind
    Practical air speeds of 95 MPH at start and
    75 MPH at end   4,210 miles

PROBABLE MAXIMUM AIR SPEED AT SEA LEVEL

Developed from calculated and clocked speeds   124 MPH

TAKE-OFF DISTANCE WITH 450 GAL. FUEL

Estimated for hard ground with zero wind at 485 ft.
elevation by extrapolation of Sec. C test data plotted   2,500 ft.

SECTION G — TOTAL POSSIBLE RANGE BY USING FUEL REMAINING IN TANKS WHEN *Spirit of St. Louis* REACHED PARIS

Fuel remaining in tanks	85 gal.
Additional range available with zero wind, practical economic air speeds	1,040 miles
Total range Practical economic air speeds for remaining fuel (3610 plus 1040)	4,650 miles

SECTION H — MAN HOURS TO DESIGN AND BUILD THE *Spirit of St. Louis*

ENGINEERING

Total time spent by the engineer (Hall) on design, weight and balance analysis, stress analysis drawings, inspection, performance analysis, and flight test engineering — Feb. 25 to May 10 (Lindbergh left San Diego)	775 man hrs.
The purchasing agent (Locke) assisted in the weight and balance analysis, and the factory manager (Bowlus) assisted in the fuel and oil system layout	75 man hrs.
TOTAL ENGINEERING	850 man hrs.

CONSTRUCTION

Total time in the construction and assembly but not including the shop superintendent's factory managers time	3,000 man hrs.

SECTION I — CONCLUDING REMARKS

A combination of factors associated with the design and construction of the *Spirit of St. Louis* made it possible to complete the project in two months. One of these was the constant availability of Lindbergh to discuss the problems which arose. Normally the purchaser of a custom-built airplane did not stay at the factory during its development, and this required to maintain an extensive correspondence. Rather complete preliminary design drawings and data had to be specially prepared and forwarded to the purchaser for study and comment. Such work and correspondence took a large part of the engineer's time. Fortunately, this was not the case for the NYP.

The presence of Charles Lindbergh, with his keen knowledge of flying, his understanding of engineering problems, his implicit faith in the proposed flight, and his constant application to it, was a most important factor in welding together the entire factory organization into one smoothly running team This group was unusually conscientious, co-operative, and hard working.

INDEX

W

Y

[opposite page] Sea gulls in flight photographed by Donald A. Hall. *Provided by the estate of Donald A. Hall, Sr.*

"It is my hope that SPIRIT AND CREATOR *has honored my grandfather, Donald Albert Hall, the sixty-day experiment that opened a new chapter in aviation*

and the lifelong friendship between two men who had faith in the sky and insubstantial air. " — Nova Hall, Grandson